# A PICTORIAL JOURNEY
# THRU THE OLD TESTAMENT

D0958112

# INTRODUCTION

In 1977, I completed work on the Old and New Testament volumes of the BASIC STAGES IN THE BOOK OF AGES. These two books contain a summarization of the entire Bible. They are used as the primary textbooks in the chronological coverage of the Liberty Home Bible Institute correspondence course.

Upon completion of this work, I began to sense the need for a visualized supplement to these volumes.

A PICTORIAL JOURNEY THRU THE OLD TESTAMENT and its New New Testament counterpart fulfill that need. This book should prove to be a very valuable aid in understanding the material contained in the BASIC STAGES volumes.

H.L. Willmington

# TABLE OF CONTENTS

# HEBREW BIBLE O.T. ARRANGEMENT

| LAW 5 | GENESIS, EXODUS, LEVITICUS, NUMBERS, DEUTERONOMY |
|---|---|
| PROPHETS 8 | **4 FORMER:** JOSHUA, JUDGES, SAMUEL, KINGS **4 LATTER:** ISAIAH, JEREMIAH, EZEKIEL, THE TWELVE |
| WRITINGS 11 | **3 POETICAL:** PSALMS, PROVERBS, JOB **5 ROLLS:** SONG OF SOLOMON, RUTH, LAMENTATIONS, ESTHER, ECCLESIASTES **3 HISTORICAL:** DANIEL, EZRA-NEHEMIAH, CHRONICLES |

# ENGLISH BIBLE O.T. ARRANGEMENT

| LAW 5 | • GENESIS • EXODUS • LEVITICUS • NUMBERS • DEUTERONOMY |
|---|---|
| HISTORY 12 | • JOSHUA • JUDGES • RUTH • I SAMUEL • II SAMUEL • I KINGS • II KINGS • I CHRONICLES • II CHRONICLES • EZRA • NEHEMIAH • ESTHER |
| POETRY 5 | • JOB • PSALMS • PROVERBS • ECCLESIASTES • SONG OF SOLOMON |
| PROPHECY 17 | *5 MAJOR* • ISAIAH • JEREMIAH • LAMENTATIONS • DANIEL • EZEKIEL *12 MINOR* • HOSEA • JOEL • AMOS • OBADIAH • JONAH • MICAH • NAHUM • HABAKKUK • ZEPHANIAH • HAGGAI • ZECHARIAH • MALACHI |

# OLD TESTAMENT BOOK STATISTICS

| BOOK | CHAPTERS | VERSES | WORDS |
|---|---|---|---|
| Genesis | 50 | 1,533 | 32,267 |
| Exodus | 40 | 1,213 | 32,692 |
| Leviticus | 27 | 859 | 24,546 |
| Numbers | 36 | 1,288 | 32,902 |
| Deuteronomy | 34 | 958 | 28,461 |
| Joshua | 24 | 658 | 18,858 |
| Judges | 21 | 618 | 18,976 |
| Ruth | 4 | 85 | 2,578 |
| I Samuel | 31 | 810 | 25,061 |
| II Samuel | 24 | 695 | 20,612 |
| I Kings | 22 | 816 | 24,524 |
| II Kings | 25 | 719 | 23,532 |
| I Chronicles | 29 | 941 | 20,369 |
| II Chronicles | 36 | 822 | 26,074 |
| Ezra | 10 | 280 | 7,441 |
| Nehemiah | 13 | 406 | 10,483 |
| Esther | 10 | 167 | 5,637 |
| Job | 42 | 1,070 | 10,102 |
| Psalms | 150 | 2,461 | 43,743 |
| Proverbs | 31 | 915 | 15,043 |
| Ecclesiastes | 12 | 222 | 5,584 |
| Song of Solomon | 8 | 117 | 2,661 |
| Isaiah | 66 | 1,292 | 37,044 |
| Jeremiah | 52 | 1,364 | 42,659 |
| Lamentations | 5 | 154 | 3,415 |
| Ezekiel | 48 | 1,273 | 39,407 |
| Daniel | 12 | 357 | 11,606 |
| Hosea | 14 | 197 | 5,175 |
| Joel | 3 | 73 | 2,034 |
| Amos | 9 | 146 | 4,217 |
| Obadiah | 1 | 21 | 670 |
| Jonah | 4 | 48 | 1,321 |
| Micah | 7 | 105 | 3,153 |
| Nahum | 3 | 47 | 1,285 |
| Habakkuk | 3 | 56 | 1,476 |
| Zephaniah | 3 | 53 | 1,617 |
| Haggai | 2 | 38 | 1,131 |
| Zechariah | 14 | 211 | 6,444 |
| Malachi | 4 | 55 | 1,782 |

# Old Testament Basic Stages

| | MAIN ACTORS | MAIN ACTION | |
|---|---|---|---|
| **UNDATED PAST-2165 B.C.** / *CREATION STAGE* | | CREATION | FALL |
| GEN. 1-11 → | ADAM, ABEL, ENOCH, NOAH | FLOOD | TOWER OF BABEL |

| | MAIN ACTORS | MAIN ACTION | |
|---|---|---|---|
| **2165-1804 B.C.** / *PATRIARCHAL STAGE* | | BEGINNING OF HEBREW NATION | |
| | | GIVING OF ABRAHAMIC COVENANT | |
| GEN. 12-50 → | ABRAHAM, ISAAC, JACOB, JOSEPH | JEWS MOVE INTO EGYPT | |
| JOB → | JOB, ELIPHAZ, BILDAD, ZOPHAR, ELIHU | GOD ALLOWS SATAN TO TEST JOB | |

| | MAIN ACTORS | MAIN ACTION | |
|---|---|---|---|
| **1804-1405 B.C.** / *EXODUS STAGE* | | DELIVERANCE FROM EGYPT | GIVING OF THE LAW |
| EXODUS / LEVITICUS / NUMBERS / DEUTERONOMY → | MOSES, AARON, MIRIAM, ELEAZER KORAH, BALAAM, PHINEHAS | BUILDING OF THE TABERNACLE | THE FAILURE AT KADESH-BARNEA |

3

# MAIN ACTION

## CONQUEST STAGE — 1405-1382 B.C.

**Book:** JOSHUA

**Main Actors:** JOSHUA, CALEB, RAHAB, ACHAN

**Main Action:**
- INVASION OF THE LAND
- SUBJECTION OF THE LAND
- DIVISION OF THE LAND

## JUDGES STAGE — 1382-1043 B.C.

**Books:** JUDGES / RUTH / FIRST SAM. 1-7

**Main Actors:**
- EHUD, BARAK, DEBORAH, GIDEON, JEPHTHAH, SAMPSON
- RUTH, NAOMI, BOAZ
- HANNAH, ELI, SAMUEL

**Main Action:**
- THE MINISTRY OF 12 MILITARY REFORMERS
- THE MARRIAGE OF A MOABITE GIRL
- THE PRAYER OF A MOTHER
- THE DEATH OF A PRIEST

## UNITED KINGDOM STAGE — 1043-931 B.C.

**Books:** FIRST SAM. 8-31, SECOND SAMUEL, FIRST KINGS 1-11, I CHRONICLES, II CHRONICLES 1-9, PSALMS, PROVERBS, ECCLESIASTES, SONG OF SOLOMON

**Main Actors:** SAUL, DAVID, SOLOMON, JOAB, ABNER, ABSALOM, GOLIATH, ZADOK, BATH-SHEBA, WITCH OF ENDOR, NATHAN, JONATHAN, QUEEN OF SHEBA

**Main Action:**
- THE 3-FOLD ANOINTING OF DAVID
  - IN BETHLEHEM BY SAMUEL
  - IN HEBRON BY 2 TRIBES
  - IN HEBRON BY ALL 12 TRIBES
- THE CAPTURE OF JERUSALEM BY DAVID
- THE BRINGING OF THE ARK INTO JERUSALEM
- THE GIVING OF THE DAVIDIC COVENANT
- THE CONSTRUCTION OF THE FIRST TEMPLE

## CHAOTIC KINGDOM STAGE

### 931–605 B.C.

| | MAIN ACTORS | MAIN ACTION |
|---|---|---|
| FIRST KINGS 12–22 | NORTHERN KINGS: JEROBOAM, OMRI, AHAB, JEHU, JEROBOAM II, HOSHEA | ISRAEL'S TRAGIC CIVIL WAR |
| SECOND KINGS | SOUTHERN KINGS: REHOBOAM, ASA, JEHOSHAPHAT, UZZIAH, AHAZ, HEZEKIAH, MANASSEH, JOSIAH, JEHOIAKIM, ZEDEKIAH | THE CAPTURE OF THE NORTHERN KINGDOM BY THE ASSYRIANS. |
| SECOND CHRONICLES 10–36 | ORAL PROPHETS: ELIJAH, MICAIAH, ELISHA. VARIOUS: JEZEBEL, NAAMAN, ATHALIAH | THE SALVATION OF JERUSALEM FROM THE ASSYRIANS |
| OBADIAH (850–840) | | THE GREAT PREACHING MINISTRY OF THE ORAL PROPHETS |
| JOEL (841–834) | | |
| JONAH (785–750) | | |
| AMOS (760–753) | AMAZIAH | THE GREAT PREACHING MINISTRY OF THE WRITING PROPHETS |
| HOSEA (760–700) | GOMER, JEZREEL, LO-RU-HA-MAH, LO-AM-MI | |
| ISAIAH (739–681) | | THE GIVING OF THE NEW COVENANT |
| MICAH (735–700) | | |
| NAHUM (650–620) | | |
| ZEPHANIAH (640–620) | BARUCH, GEDALIAL, ISHMAEL, JOHANAN | THE CAPTURE OF THE SOUTHERN KINGDOM BY THE BABYLONIANS |
| JEREMIAH (627–575) | | |
| HABAKKUK (609–606) | | |
| LAMENTATIONS (586) | | |

| | MAIN ACTORS | MAIN ACTION |
|---|---|---|
| **CAPTIVITY STAGE** 605-538 B.C.<br>DANIEL (605-536)<br>EZEKIEL (593-560) | DANIEL, NEBUCHADNEZZAR, SHADRACH, MESHACH, ABEDNEGO, BELSHAZZAR, DARIUS | PERSONAL DELIVERANCE OF DANIEL AND HIS FRIENDS<br>DESTRUCTION OF FIRST TEMPLE<br>DESCRIPTION OF THE FUTURE MILLENNIAL TEMPLE<br>A PANORAMA OF GENTILE WORLD POWERS<br>A PREVIEW OF ISRAEL'S FUTURE<br>THE FALL OF BABYLON |
| **RETURN STAGE** 538-400 B.C.<br>EZRA (438-440)<br>ESTHER (478-463)<br>NEHEMIAH (445-415)<br>HAGGAI (520-504)<br>ZECHARIAH (520-488)<br>MALACHI (427-400) | CYRUS, JOSHUA, ZERUBBABEL, EZRA, AHASUERUS, ESTHER, MORDECAI, HAMAN, NEHEMIAH, ARTAXERXES, SANBALLAT | THE DECREE OF CYRUS<br>THE CONSTRUCTION OF THE SECOND TEMPLE<br>THE REBUILDING OF THE WALLS<br>THE DELIVERANCE OF THE JEWS IN PERSIA |

# A DATED OLD TESTAMENT CHRONOLOGY

I.  The Creation Stage (Undated Past to 2165 B.C.)

    A.  Biblical Record:

    Genesis 1 - 11

    B.  Biblical Events:

        1.  Creation of the Heavens and Earth

        2.  The Fall

        3.  The Flood

        4.  The Tower of Babel

II.  The Patriarchal Stage:  (2165 B.C. to 1804 B.C.)

    A.  Biblical Record:

        1.  Genesis 12 - 50

        2.  Job

    B.  Biblical Events:

        1.  2165 B.C. - The Birth of Abram (Genesis 11:26)

        2.  2090 - Abram enters Canaan (Genesis 12)

        3.  2079 - Birth of Ishmael (Genesis 16)

        4.  2066 - Destruction of Sodom (Genesis 19)

        5.  2065 - Birth of Isaac (Genesis 21)

        6.  2045?- Sacrifice of Isaac on Mt. Moriah (Genesis 22)

        7.  2028 - Death of Sarah (Genesis 23)

        8.  2025 - Marriage of Isaac and Rebekah (Genesis 24)

        9.  2005 - Birth of Esau and Jacob (Genesis 25)

      10.  1990 - Death of Abraham (Genesis 25)

      11.  1990? - Life of Job (Book of Job)

      12.  1985? - Esau sells his birthright to Jacob (Genesis 25)

      13.  1928 - Jacob deceives his father Isaac and flees to Haran. (Genesis 27)

      14.  1914 - Birth of Joseph (Genesis 30)

      15.  1908 - Return of Jacob to Shechem (Genesis 33)

16.  1898 - Return of Jacob to Bethel (Genesis 35)

17.  1897 - Joseph is sold into Egypt (Genesis 37)

18.  1884 - Joseph is exalted by the Pharaoh (Genesis 41)

19.  1875 - Jacob and his family enter Egypt (Genesis 46)

20.  1858 - The death of Jacob (Genesis 49)

21.  1804 - The death of Joseph (Genesis 50)


III.  The Exodus Stage (1804 - 1405)

A.  Biblical Record:

1.  Exodus

2.  Leviticus

3.  Numbers

4.  Deuteronomy

B.  Biblical Events:

1.  1804 - 1730.  Israel enjoys prosperity for 75 years after the death
    of Joseph (Exodus 1:1-7)

2.  1730 - Egyptian oppression begins (Exodus 1:8-12:42)

3.  1525 - Birth of Moses (Exodus 2:1-4)

4.  1485 - Moses flees Egypt (Exodus 2:11-15)

5.  1445 - Moses returns to Egypt (Exodus 4:20)

6.  April 14, 1445 - Passover is instituted (Exodus 12:2)

7.  May 15, 1445 - Giving of the Manna (Exodus 16:14)

8.  June 15, 1445 - Arrival at Mt. Sinai (Exodus 19:1)

9.  April 1, 1444 - Completion of the Tabernacle (Exodus 40)

10.  May 20, 1444 - Departure for Kadesh-barnea (Numbers 10:11)

11.  August, 1444 - Encampment at Kadesh - barnea (Numbers 13:1-14:45)

12.  1444 - 1405 - Wandering in Wilderness (Number 15:1 - Deut. 34)

13.  April, 1405 - Death of Miriam (Numbers 20:1)

14.  August 1405 - Death of Aaron (Numbers 20:28)

15.  October ?, 1405 - Death of Moses (Deut. 34:1-7)

IV.  The Conquest Stage (1405 - 1382 B.C.)

    A.  Biblical Record:

        Joshua

    B.  Biblical Events:

        1.  April 10, 1404 - The Crossing of Jordan (Josh.1-5)

        2.  1404-1397 - The Conquering of the Land (Josh. 6-12)

        3.  1390 - The death of Joshua (Josh. 23-24)

        4.  1382 - Death of the surviving elders (Josh. 24:31)

V.  The Judges Stage (1382 - 1043 B.C.)

    A.  Biblical Record:

        1.  Judges

        2.  Ruth

        3.  First Samuel 1 - 7

    B.  Biblical Events:

        1.  1237-Deborah and Barak (Judgest 4 - 5)

        2.  1191 - Gideon (Judges 6 - 8)

        3.  1150-Ruth (Book of Ruth)

        4.  1107 - Ministry of Eli  (1 Samuel 1 - 4)

        5.  1087 - Jephthah (Judges 11-12)

        6.  1069 - Samson (Judges 13-16)

        7.  1067 - Ministry of Samuel (1 Samuel 1 - 8)

VI.  The United Kingdom Stage (1043-931 - B.C.)

    A.  Biblical Record:

        1.  First Samuel 8 - 31

        2.  Second Samuel

        3.  First Kings 1 - 11

        4.  First Chronicles

        5.  Second Chronicles 1 - 9

        6.  Psalms

        7.  Proverbs

        8.  Ecclesiastes

        9.  Song of Solomon

    B.  Biblical Event:

        1.  1043 - Saul is anointed (1 Samuel 10)

        2.  1040 - Birth of David

        3.  1025 - The anointing of David (1 Samuel 16)

        4.  1020 ? -  David and Goliath (1 Samuel 17)

        5.  1011 - Death of Saul (1 Samuel 31)

        6.  1011 - Reign of David over two tribes (2 Samuel 2:4)

        7.  1004 - Reign of David over all Israel  (2 Samuel 5:1)

        8.  1005 - Jerusalem becomes the capital (2 Samuel 5:6)

        9.   990 - David and Bathsheba (2 Samuel 11)

       10.   979 - Revolt of Absalom (2 Samuel 15 - 18)

       11.   971 - Death of David (1 Kings 2)

       12.   971 - Reign of Solomon (1 Kings 1:39)

       13.  April, 966 - Beginning of Temple Construction (1 Kings 6:1)

       14.  October, 959 - Completion of Temple (1 Kings 6:38)

       15.  931 - Death of Solomon (1 Kings 11:43)

VII. The Chaotic Kingdom Stage (931-605 B.C.)

A. Biblical Record:

   1. First Kings 12 - 22

   2. Second Kings

   3. Second Chronicles 10 - 36

   4. Obadiah (850-840)

   5. Joel (841-834)

   6. Jonah (785-750)

   7. Amos (760-753)

   8. Hosea (760-700)

   9. Isaiah (739-681)

   10. Micah (735-700)

   11. Nahum (650-620)

   12. Zephaniah (640-620)

   13. Jeremiah (627-575)

   14. Habakkuk (609-606)

   15. Lamentations (586)

B. Biblical Events

   1. 931 - The Tragic Civil War (1 Kings 12)

   2. 911 - The reign of Asa, Judah's first saved king (2 Chron. 14-16)

   3. 874 - The reign of Ahab (1 Kings 16 - 22)

   4. 873 - The reign of Jehoshaphat (2 Chron. 17-20)

   5. 860-852 - The ministry of Elijah (1 Kings 17-19,21; 2 Kings 1-2)

   6. 852-795 - The ministry of Elisha (2 Kings 2-9,13)

   7. 848 - The ministry of Obadiah.

   8. 835 - The ministry of Joel.

   9. 800 - The ministry of Jonah.

   10. 760 - The ministry of Amos.

11

11.  760 - The ministry of Hosea

12.  735 - The ministry of Micah.

13.  721 - The capture of the Northern Kingdom (2 Kings 17)

14.  716 - The reign of Hezekiah (2 Chron. 29 - 32)

15.  701 - Jerusalem saved by the death angel (2 Kings 19)

16.  697 - The reign of Manasseh (2 Chron. 33)

17.  664 - The ministry of Nahum.

18.  641 - The reign of Josiah (2 Chron. 34, 35)

19.  640 - The ministry of Zephaniah.

20.  627 - The ministry of Jeremiah.

21.  626 - The beginning of the Neo-Babylonian Empire.

22.  612 - The fall of Nineveh (book of Nahum)

23.  609 - The ministry of Habakkuk.

24.  605 - The battle of Carchemish (Jeremiah 46:2)

25.  605 - The first siege of Jerusalem, Daniel taken (2 Kings 24)

26.  597 - The reign of Zedekiah (2 Chronicles 36)

27.  597 - The second siege of Jerusalem, Ezekiel taken (2 Kings 24)

28.  July 18, 586 - The third siege of Jerusalem, temple burned (2 Kings 24)

29.  586 - The book of Lamentations.


VIII.  The Captivity Stage (605 - 538 B.C.)

   A.  Biblical Record:

      1.  Daniel

      2.  Ezekiel

   B.  Biblical Events:

1. 605-536 - The ministry of Daniel

2. 593-560 - The ministry of Ezekiel

3. 550 - Cyrus organizes the Persian Empire.

4. October 29, 539 - The fall of Babylon (Daniel 5)

5. 538 - The edict of Cyrus (Ezra 1)

IX. The Return Stage (538-400)

A. Biblical Record:

1. Ezra (458-440)

2. Esther (478-463)

3. Nehemiah (445-415)

4. Haggai (520-504)

5. Zechariah (520-488)

6. Malachi (437-400)

B. Biblical Events:

1. 536 - First return under Zerubbabel (Ezra 1 - 6)

2. June, 535 - Work on the temple begun (Ezra 3)

3. 520 - Ministry of Haggai (Ezra 5:1; Book of Haggai)

4. 520 - Ministry of Zechariah (Ezra 5:1; Book of Zechariah)

5. Feb. 18, 516 - Work on temple completed (Ezra 6:15)

6. 478 - Esther becomes queen (Esther 2)

7. March, 455 - Second return under Ezra (Ezra 7-10)

8. April, 445 - Return under Nehemiah (Neh. 2)

9. Sept., 445 - The walls are completed (Neh. 6:15)

10. 437 - Ministry of Malachi.

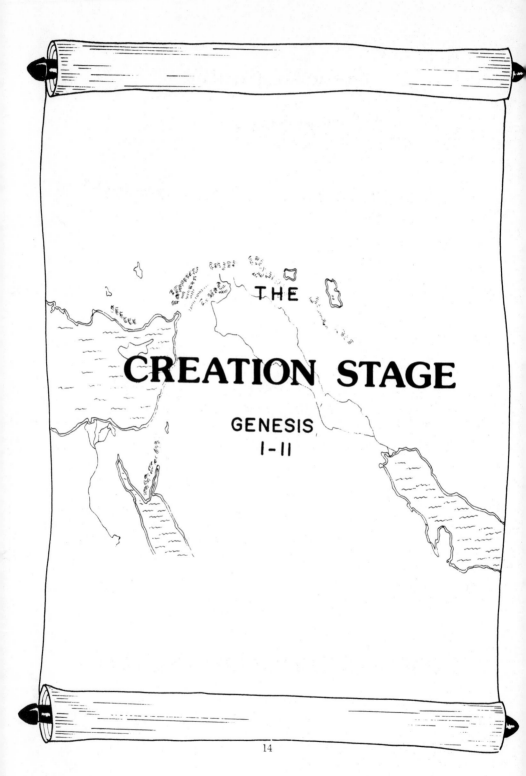

# THE CREATION STAGE

### GENESIS 1-11

# "In the Beginning

# GOD

# Created the Heaven and the Earth"

| | | |
|---|---|---|
| • THIS IS A SUMMARIZA-TION STATEMENT | 1:1 | TELLS US **WHAT** GOD DID . |
| | 1:2-2:25 | TELLS US **HOW** HE DID IT. |
| • THIS IS A REFUTATION STATEMENT | PHILOSOPHY REFUTED | HOW REFUTED |
| | ATHEISM | THERE IS A GOD |
| | POLYTHEISM | THERE IS BUT ONE GOD |
| | EVOLUTION | HE CREATED ALL THINGS |
| | PANTHEISM | HE IS APART FROM HIS CREATION |
| | MATERIALISM | THERE WAS A BEGINNING TO CREATION |
| | FATALISM | THERE WAS A PURPOSE TO CREATION |

# THE WONDERS OF GEN. 1:1

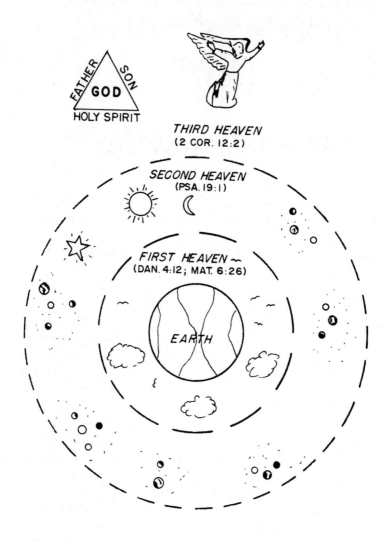

# THE THREE HEAVENS OF CREATION

(SEE GEN. 1:1; 2:1)

16

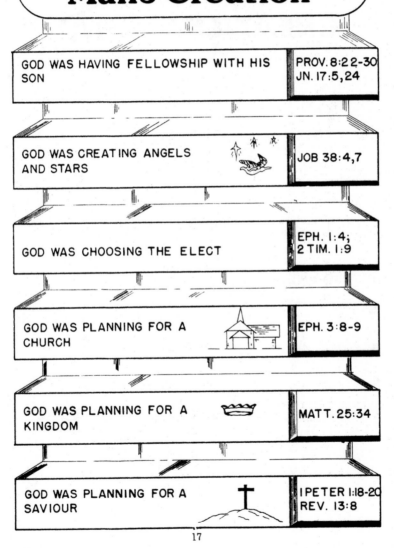

# GOD'S Activities
## Prior
## to
# Man's Creation

| | |
|---|---|
| GOD WAS HAVING FELLOWSHIP WITH HIS SON | PROV. 8:22-30 JN. 17:5,24 |
| GOD WAS CREATING ANGELS AND STARS | JOB 38:4,7 |
| GOD WAS CHOOSING THE ELECT | EPH. 1:4; 2 TIM. 1:9 |
| GOD WAS PLANNING FOR A CHURCH | EPH. 3:8-9 |
| GOD WAS PLANNING FOR A KINGDOM | MATT. 25:34 |
| GOD WAS PLANNING FOR A SAVIOUR | I PETER 1:18-20 REV. 13:8 |

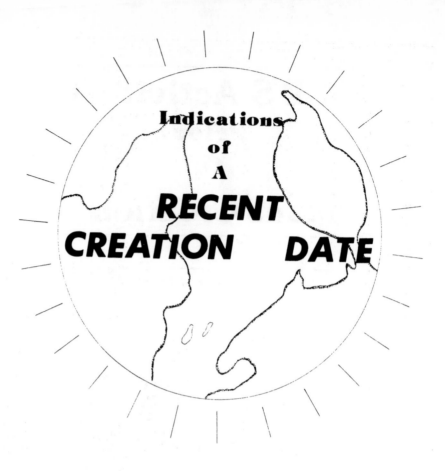

**Indications of A RECENT CREATION DATE**

- ● POPULATION STATISTICS

- ⬡ THE AMOUNT OF HELIUM-4 IN THE ATMOSPHERE

- ● THE ABSENCE OF METEORITE DUST

- ⬡ THE DECAY OF EARTH'S MAGNETIC FIELD

- ● THE IMBALANCE OF CARBON-14 AND CARBON-12

| CREATION | CORRUPTION | CONDEMNATION | CONFUSION |
|---|---|---|---|
| ORIGIN OF ALL THINGS | SIN OF ADAM | FLOOD OF NOAH | TOWER OF BABEL |
| ● SIX DAYS OF CREATION | ● SUBTLETY OF SATAN | ● CONDITIONS BEFORE THE FLOOD | ● THE ARROGANCE OF MAN |
| ● ONE DAY OF REST | ● SIN OF ADAM | ● SALVATION THROUGH THE FLOOD | ● THE JUDGMENT OF GOD |
| | ● REDEMPTION OF ABEL | ● THE TRAGEDY AFTER THE FLOOD | ● THE ORIGIN OF NATIONS |
| | ● MINISTRY OF ENOCH | | |
| GEN. 1-2 | GEN. 3-5 | GEN. 6-9 | GEN. 10-11 |

GENESIS 1-11

IN The Beginning GOD

19

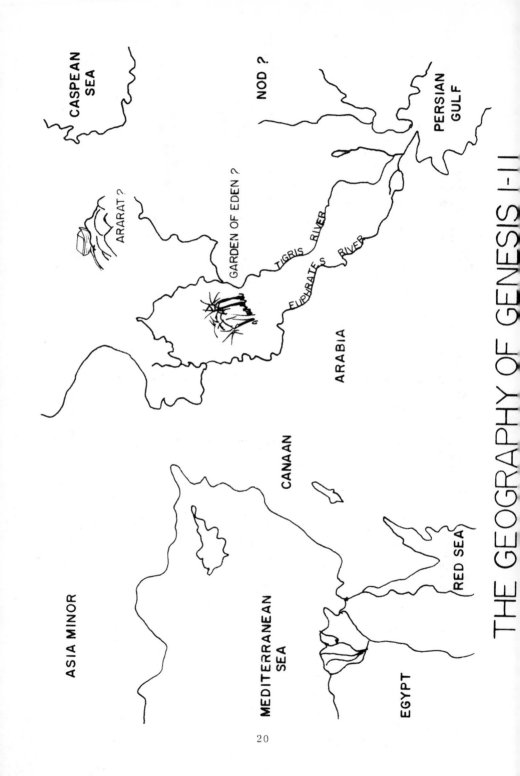

THE GEOGRAPHY OF GENESIS I-II

# The Creation Week

| DAY | FIRST DAY | SECOND DAY | THIRD DAY | FOURTH DAY | FIFTH DAY | SIXTH DAY | SEVENTH DAY |
|---|---|---|---|---|---|---|---|
| **ACTION** | CREATION OF Earth, Light and probably Angels. | SEPARATION OF the Upper and Lower Waters by space. | CREATION OF Plant Life | CREATION OF the Sun, Moon, and Stars. | CREATION OF Fish and Fowl | CREATION OF Land Animals and Man | CREATION COMPLETED. GOD RESTS |
| **COMMENT** | A. Created Universe now Energized. B. Earth's Rotation on its Axis begins C. Gravitational, Electro-magnetic and Nuclear Force fields now in effect. | A. Upper Atmosphere may have had more water vapor than today. B. Would help explain longevity before the FLOOD. C. Would help explain the FLOOD itself. | A. Totally refutes Theistic Evolution. B. Darwin said life began in Ancient Ocean. C. MOSES said it began on Dry Ground. | Why was the EARTH Created before the SUN? A. TO SHOW GOD'S PRIORITY. B. To prevent Sun worship. | A. Included the Tiny Humming Bird. B. Included the mighty Blue Sperm Whale. | Included ALL Land Animals from the doggy to the Dinosaur. | A. The 7th day Now becomes A SYMBOL of a Finished CREATION. B. Only Time GOD is pictured as Resting. |

# The DAYS of CREATION

- **THE LENGTH OF THESE DAYS**

  QUESTION: ARE THESE LITERAL 24-HOUR DAYS?

  ANSWER: YES, BECAUSE OF THE FOLLOWING REASONS.

| | |
|---|---|
| 1. | THE NUMERICAL ADJECTIVE USED WITH WORD DAY (HEB., YOM) INDICATES THIS. |
| 2. | MOSES BELIEVED IT (EXOD. 20:11; 31:17) |
| 3. | DAVID BELIEVED IT (PSA. 33:6-9) |
| 4. | MOST HEBREW LANGUAGE SCHOLARS BELIEVE IT. |
| 5. | HEBREW STRUCTURE ITSELF SEEMS TO TEACH IT. |

- **THE CORRELATION OF THESE DAYS**

  FIRST 3 DAYS  PROVIDE THE BACKDROP FOR THE CREATION DRAMA

  LAST 3 DAYS  PROVIDE THE ACTUAL ACTORS IN THE CREATION DRAMA

| THE BACKDROP | | THE ACTORS | |
|---|---|---|---|
| DAY ONE | LIGHT | DAY FOUR | SUN, MOON, AND STARS |
| DAY TWO | FIRMAMENT AND WATER | DAY FIVE | FOWL AND FISH |
| DAY THREE | LAND AND VEGETATION | DAY SIX | ANIMALS AND MAN |

- **THE TWO-FOLD ACCOUNT OF THESE DAYS**

| THE FLOODLIGHT ACCOUNT (GEN. 1) | THE SPOTLIGHT ACCOUNT (GEN. 2) |
|---|---|
| A GENERAL DESCRIPTION OF THE CREATION OF THE UNIVERSE. | A SPECIFIC DESCRIPTION OF THE CREATION OF MAN |
| A CHRONOLOGICAL ACCOUNT | A TOPICAL ACCOUNT |

# THE GAP THEORY

| MEANING OF | • IN GEN. 1:1 GOD CREATED A PERFECT AND COMPLETE UNIVERSE. |
| | • BETWEEN 1:1 AND 1:2 SATAN'S REBELLION MARRED THIS PERFECT UNIVERSE. |
| | • FROM 1:2 ON GOD REMOLDS THIS SIN-MARRED CREATION. |

| POPULARITY OF | MADE POPULAR AND WELL KNOWN BY TWO MEN: |
| | • GEORGE H. PEMBER IN 1876 |
| | • C.I. SCOFIELD IN 1917 |

| CONSIDERATION OF | ARGUMENTS FOR GAP THEORY | ARGUMENTS AGAINST GAP THEORY |
|---|---|---|
| GOD SAYS / MAN SAYS | • WORDS "Without form and void" Always indicate Judgment. See ISA. 34:11; 45:18; Jer. 4:23 | • FALSE. Words can often simply refer to Lifelessness and Empty Space. See JOB 26:7; Deut. 32:10 |
| | • VERB "WAS" in 1:2 Should be translated "BECAME" | • FALSE. Heb. word Hayetha (was) is almost always as "was". It is used 264 times in the Pentateuch. Of these, it is translated "was" 258 times. See Jonah 3:3 for an example. |
| | • THERE IS A DIFFERENCE BETWEEN CREATED (BARA) AND MADE (ASAH) | • FALSE. Words are used interchangeably EXAMPLE: 1. GOD Created (Bara) the great sea monsters (1:21) 2. GOD made (Asah) the beast of the earth. (1:15) 3. "Let us make (Asah) man " (1:26) 4. "So GOD Created (Bara) man" (1:27) |
| | • WORD "DARKNESS" INDICATES JUDGMENT. SEE 1:2 | • FALSE. Darkness here is simply the absence of light and is sometimes spoken of as being good. See Psa. 104:20, 24 |
| | • WORD "REPLENISH" IN 1:28 INDICATES THE WORLD WAS ONCE FILLED. | • FALSE. Heb. word "MALE" almost always means simply to fill. See Exod. 40:34; 1KINGS 18:33; PSA. 107:9 |

# THE 3-FOLD PROBLEM OF THE GAP THEORY

## IT IS UNSCIENTIFIC

▲ THE GAP THEORY WAS (IN PART) A CHRISTIAN ATTEMPT TO RECONCILE THE CREATION ACCOUNT WITH THE LONG PERIODS OF TIME IN THE THEORY OF EVOLUTION.

▲ BUT EVOLUTION ITSELF AS A THEORY IS TOTALLY UNSCIENTIFIC, DEFYING THE SECOND LAW OF THERMODYNAMICS.

## IT IS UNSCRIPTURAL

⬢ THE GAP THEORY WOULD DESCRIBE ADAM WALKING ATOP A GIGANTIC FOSSILIZED ANIMAL GRAVEYARD.

⬢ PAUL, HOWEVER, IN ROM. 5:12 AND 8:20-22 STATES THAT MAN'S SIN BROUGHT ABOUT DEATH, EVEN OF ANIMALS!

## IT IS UNNECESSARY

● THE MOST NATURAL INTERPRETATION OF GEN. 1 AND 2 IS TAKING IT AT FACE VALUE, WITHOUT ADDITION OR SUBSTRACTION.

● GEN. 1:1 THUS BECOMES A SUMMARY STATEMENT OF CREATION.
1. IN THE FIRST VERSE GOD TELLS US WHAT HE DID!
2. IN THE REMAINING VERSES HE TELLS US HOW HE DID IT!

# THREE VIEWS ON THE ORIGIN OF LIFE

| BELIEF | ATHEISTIC MATERIALISM | THEISTIC EVOLUTION | SPECIAL CREATION |
|---|---|---|---|
| SOURCE | Accidental Arrangement of Molecules | GOD Through Evolution | GOD in Six Literal Days |
| TIME | ONE BILLION YEARS AGO | ONE BILLION YEARS AGO | LESS THAN 10,000 YEARS |
| METHOD | MUTATIONS | MUTATIONS | SUPERNATURAL ACT FROM THE HAND OF GOD |
| PURPOSE | NO PURPOSE | TO GLORIFY GOD | TO GLORIFY GOD |
| FIRST MAN | Some Remote Sub Human Male APE | Some Remote Sub Human Male APE | ADAM |
| FIRST WOMAN | Some Remote Sub Human Female APE | Some Remote Sub Human Female APE | EVE |
| VIEW OF GEN. 1-3 ; ROM. 5: 12-21 | PURE MYTH | SPIRITUAL ALLEGORY | HISTORICAL FACT |
| PROPONENT | DARWIN AND HIS FOLLOWERS | THOSE WHO WOULD ATTEMPT TO RECONCILE MOSES AND DARWIN | MOSES |
| REASON FOR VIEW | CONTEMPT FOR SUPERNATURAL POSSIBILITY | MISTAKEN VIEW THAT EVOLUTION HAS BEEN PROVEN AND MUST BE ACCEPTED | LITERAL INTERPRETATION OF GEN. 1; 2 |
| PROBLEM | 1st Law of Thermodynamics 2nd Law of Thermodynamics Law of Bio-Genesis | Cannot Take at FACE VALUE - GEN. 1-2; ROM. 5: 12-21 | NO REAL PROBLEM |
| SCRIPTURAL PROOF | NONE | NONE | GEN. 1:31; 2:1-3; EX. 20:11 31:17; PSA. 33:6-9; I COR. 11:8-9; 15:39; I TIM. 2:13 |
| SCIENTIFIC SUPPORT | NONE | NONE | 1st Law of Thermodynamics, 2d Law of Thermodynamics, Law of Bio-Genesis |

ATHEISTIC

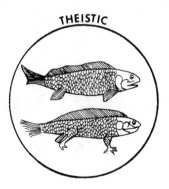

THEISTIC

CREATION

SEVEN FACTS ABOUT ADAM

* THE HIGHLIGHT OF GOD'S CREATION

*ABSOLUTELY UNIQUE

*MADE IN GOD'S IMAGE

*DECLARED KING OF CREATION

*COMMANDED NOT TO EAT OF THE TREE OF THE KNOWLEDGE OF GOOD AND EVIL

* ENCOURAGED TO EAT OF ALL OTHER TREES

*GIVEN A WIFE

# FIVE-FOLD JUDGMENT UPON SIN

## (GENESIS 3)

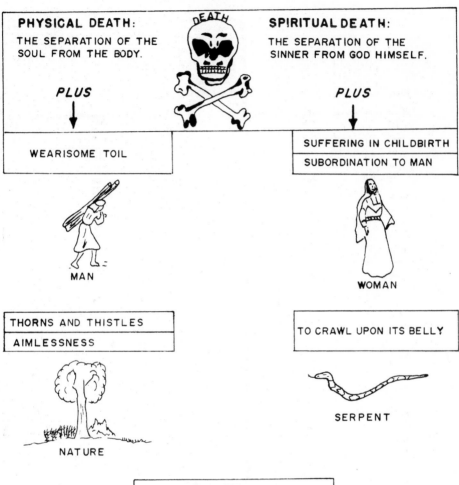

**PHYSICAL DEATH:**
THE SEPARATION OF THE SOUL FROM THE BODY.

*PLUS*

WEARISOME TOIL

MAN

**SPIRITUAL DEATH:**
THE SEPARATION OF THE SINNER FROM GOD HIMSELF.

*PLUS*

SUFFERING IN CHILDBIRTH

SUBORDINATION TO MAN

WOMAN

THORNS AND THISTLES

AIMLESSNESS

NATURE

TO CRAWL UPON ITS BELLY

SERPENT

TO SUFFER A FATAL HEAD WOUND

SATAN

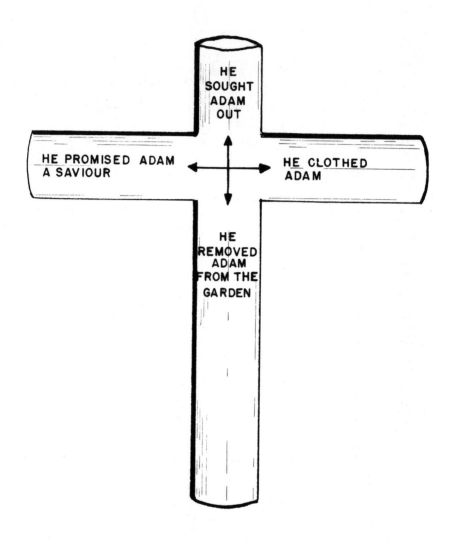

On the cross:

HE
SOUGHT
ADAM
OUT

HE PROMISED ADAM
A SAVIOUR

HE CLOTHED
ADAM

HE
REMOVED
ADAM
FROM THE
GARDEN

## —THE FOUR FOLD GRACE OF GOD —

(GENESIS 3)

# THE VICIOUS VOCABULARY OF SIN

## AS INTRODUCED BY THE FIRST ADAM

BY GEN. 2:17  *HE INTRODUCED* ..... DEATH

BY GEN. 3:17  *HE INTRODUCED* ..... NAKEDNESS

BY GEN. 3:14  *HE INTRODUCED* ..... CURSE

BY GEN. 3:17  *HE INTRODUCED* ..... SORROW

BY GEN. 3:18  *HE INTRODUCED* ..... THORNS

BY GEN. 3:19  *HE INTRODUCED* ..... SWEAT

BY GEN. 3:24  *HE INTRODUCED* ..... SWORD

## AS DEALT WITH BY THE SECOND ADAM

BY HEB. 2:9  *HE DEALT WITH* ..... DEATH

BY JOHN 19:23  *HE DEALT WITH* ..... NAKEDNESS

BY GAL. 3:13  *HE DEALT WITH* ..... CURSE

BY ISA. 53:3  *HE DEALT WITH* ..... SORROW

BY JOHN 19:5  *HE DEALT WITH* ..... THORNS

BY LK. 22:44  *HE DEALT WITH* ..... SWEAT

BY JOHN 19:34  *HE DEALT WITH* ..... SWORD

## HIS SENTENCE

TO ENDURE BURDENSOME TOIL
AS A WANDERING FUGITIVE
WITHOUT PEACE OR PURPOSE.

## HIS CIVILIZATION

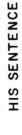

- HE BUILDS THE FIRST CITY

- HIS DESCENDENTS BECOME THE
  INVENTORS OF THE TENT,
  NOMADIC LIFE STYLE, MUSIC
  AND METALLURGY.

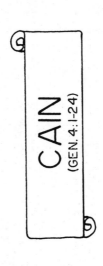

# CAIN
### (GEN. 4:1-24)

## HIS SIN

WAS THE WORLD'S FIRST
MODERNIST.

WAS THE WORLD'S FIRST
MURDERER

## HIS SPOUSE

- QUESTION : WHERE DID CAIN
  GET HIS WIFE ?

- ANSWER : HE DOUBTLESS
  MARRIED ONE OF
  HIS SISTERS.
  SEE GEN. 5:4

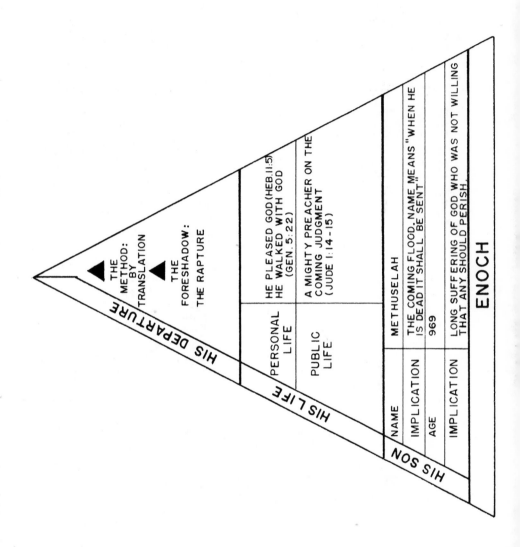

ENOCH

HIS DEPARTURE

THE METHOD: BY TRANSLATION

THE FORESHADOW: THE RAPTURE

HIS LIFE

| PERSONAL LIFE | HE PLEASED GOD (HEB. 11:5) HE WALKED WITH GOD (GEN. 5:22) |
| PUBLIC LIFE | A MIGHTY PREACHER ON THE COMING JUDGMENT (JUDE 1:14-15) |

HIS SON

| NAME | METHUSELAH |
| IMPLICATION | THE COMING FLOOD. NAME MEANS "WHEN HE IS DEAD IT SHALL BE SENT" |
| AGE | 969 |
| IMPLICATION | LONG SUFFERING OF GOD WHO WAS NOT WILLING THAT ANY SHOULD PERISH. |

| VIEW ONE | VIEW TWO |
|---|---|
| WERE SIMPLY CARNAL MEN FROM LINE OF SETH | WERE ACTUALLY FALLEN ANGELS |
| • THIS THE MOST NATURAL WAY TO INTERPRET THE PASSAGE. | • THE HEBREW LANGUAGE SEEMS TO FAVOR IT.<br><br>I. HEB. PHRASE *BNE-ELOHIM* (SONS OF GOD) ALWAYS REFERS TO ANGELS IN THE O.T. SEE JOB 1:6; 2:1; 38:7; DAN. 3:25. |
| • BECAUSE OF THE STATEMENT IN MATT. 22:30 ABOUT ANGELS. | 2. HEB. WORD *NEPHILIM* (TRANS-LATED "GIANTS" IN 6:4) SHOULD BE RENDERED, "FALLEN ONES" |
| • BECAUSE OF THE STATEMENT IN I COR. 15:38-40 ABOUT ANGELS. | • BECAUSE OF ANCIENT PAGAN LEGENDS OF INDIVIDUALS WHO WERE HALF MAN, HALF GOD (EXAMPLE GILGAMESH). MOST LEGENDS USUALLY BASED ON SOME TRUTH. |
| • BECAUSE THE REGULAR HEBREW WORD FOR ANGEL IS *MALEK,* AND IS NOT USED BY MOSES HERE. | • BECAUSE MOST JEWISH SCHOLARS HAVE HELD THIS. |
| • BECAUSE OF THE LAW OF BIOGEN-ESIS. SEE GEN 1:11, "AFTER ITS KIND." | • BECAUSE THE EARLY CHURCH HELD IT. |
| • BECAUSE IT WOULD COMPROMISE THE CONCEPT OF THE VIRGIN BIRTH. | • BECAUSE OF THE PASSAGE IN I PETER 3:18-20 |
| | • BECAUSE THERE EXISTS TWO KINDS OF FALLEN ANGELS.<br><br>I. CHAINED. SEE 2 PETER 2:4; JUDE 1:5-7<br>2. UNCHAINED. SEE EPH. 6:12; LK. 8:27; MARK 1:23 |
| | • BECAUSE ONLY 8 HUMAN BEINGS WERE SAVED FROM THE GREAT FLOOD. |

# TWO VIEWS ON THE SONS OF GOD IN GEN. 6

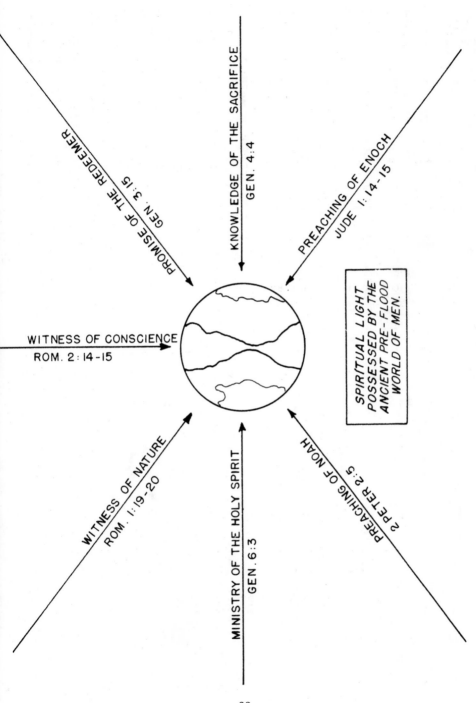

KNOWLEDGE OF THE SACRIFICE
GEN. 4:4

PROMISE OF THE REDEEMER
GEN. 3:15

PREACHING OF ENOCH
JUDE 1: 14-15

WITNESS OF CONSCIENCE
ROM. 2 : 14-15

SPIRITUAL LIGHT
POSSESSED BY THE
ANCIENT PRE-FLOOD
WORLD OF MEN.

WITNESS OF NATURE
ROM. 1: 19-20

MINISTRY OF THE HOLY SPIRIT
GEN. 6:3

PREACHING OF NOAH
2 PETER 2:5

# PHYSICAL FEATURES AND MORAL FAILURES OF THE ANCIENT WORLD

## THE PHYSICAL FEATURES

- UNIVERSALLY WARM WITH PLEASANT AND MILD CLIMATE.
- NO DESERTS OR ICE CAPS
- MORE LAND SURFACE THAN TODAY
- SMALLER AND SHALLOWER OCEAN BASINS
- NO RUGGED MOUNTAINS OR DEEP CANYONS
- CONSTANT GENTLE WEATHER CONDITIONS
- WORLD WIDE LUSH VEGETATION
- NO RAINFALL. EARTH PROBABLY WATERED BY GROUND DEWS AND FROM ARTISIAN SPRINGS.

## THE MORAL FAILURES

- PREOCCUPATION WITH PHYSICAL APPETITES (LK. 17:27)
- RAPID ADVANCES IN TECHNOLOGY (GEN. 4:22)
- GROSSLY MATERIALISTIC ATTITUDES AND INTERESTS (LK. 17:28)
- UNIFORMITARIAN PHILOSOPHIES (HEB. 11:7; 2 PET. 3:4)
- INODINATE DEVOTION TO PLEASURE AND COMFORT (GEN. 4:21)
- NO CONCERN FOR GOD IN EITHER BELIEF OR CONDUCT (2 PETER 2:4; JUDE 15)
- DISREGARD FOR THE SACREDNESS OF MARRIAGE RELATIONSHIP (MATT. 24:38)
- REJECTION OF THE INSPIRED WORD OF GOD (I PET. 3:19)
- POPULATION EXPLOSION (GEN. 6:1, 11)
- WIDESPREAD VIOLENCE (GEN. 6:11, 13)
- CORRUPTION THROUGHOUT SOCIETY (GEN. 6:12)
- PREOCCUPATION WITH ILLICIT SEX ACTIVITY (GEN. 4:19; 6:2)
- WIDESPREAD WORDS AND THOUGHTS OF BLASPHEMY (JUDE 1:15)
- ORGANIZED SATANIC ACTIVITY (GEN. 6:1-4)
- PROMULGATION OF SYSTEMS AND MOVEMENTS OF ABNORMAL DEPRAVITY (GEN. 6:5, 12)

# FLOOD FACTS

| | |
|---|---|
| ● WHEN DID THE FLOOD BEGIN ? | IT BEGAN IN NOVEMBER. THIS MONTH IS LAMENTED BY MANY PEOPLE AROUND THE WORLD AS THE DAY OF THE DEAD |
| ● HOW LONG DID THE FLOOD LAST ? | 371 DAYS |

| | | |
|---|---|---|
| ● WHAT MAY HAVE TRIGGERED THE FLOOD ? | A. | AN EARTHQUAKE MAY HAVE RELEASED VAST AND PRESSURED WATER RESERVOIRS IN THE EARTH'S MANTLE (GEN: 7:11) |
| | B. | THIS MAY HAVE BLOWN IMMENSE AMOUNTS OF DUST SKYWARD WHICH WOULD THEN INITIATE THE CONDENSATION AND PRECIPITATION OF THE WATERY CANOPY. |
| ● WAS THE FLOOD WORLD-WIDE ? YES! | A. | BECAUSE OF THE NEED FOR THE ARK. |
| | B. | BECAUSE OF THE WIDE DISTRIBUTION OF MAN BEFORE THE FLOOD. SEE GEN. 4:16 |
| | C. | BECAUSE OF THE COMPARISON MADE IN 2 PETER 3:3-7 |
| | D. | BECAUSE OF THE UNIVERSAL FLOOD TRADITIONS |
| | E. | BECAUSE OF THE MARINE FOSSILS FOUND ON MOUNTAINS |
| | F. | BECAUSE OF THE MANY FOSSIL FISH BEDS |
| | G. | BECAUSE OF THE WORLD-WIDE ANIMAL FOSSIL GRAVEYARDS |
| | H. | BECAUSE OF THE EVIDENCE OF RECENT WATER BODIES IN PRESENT DESERT AREAS. |
| | I. | BECAUSE OF THE EVIDENCE OF RECENT DRASTIC RISE IN THE SEA LEVEL. |
| | J. | BECAUSE OF THE EVIDENCE FROM THE GEOLOGIC COLUMN |
| ● HOW BIG WAS THE ARK ? | A. | 450 FEET LONG, 75 FEET WIDE, 45 FEET HIGH. |
| | B. | HAD A TOTAL DECK OF 97,700 SQUARE FEET. (EQUIVALENT TO 20 STANDARD COLLEGE BASKET-BALL COURTS) |
| | C. | LARGEST SHIP EVER BUILT UNTIL 1884 A.D. |
| | D. | NEARLY ONE HALF THE LENGTH OF THE QUEEN MARY. |
| ● HOW DID NOAH FIND ROOM FOR ALL THE ANIMALS ? | A. | TOTAL ANIMAL POPULATION WOULD NOT HAVE EXCEEDED 35,000 VERTEBRATES. |
| | B. | AVERAGE SIZE WOULD BE THAT OF A SHEEP |
| | C. | MODERN TRAIN OF 150 BOX CARS COULD CARRY THIS |
| | D. | ARK HAD CARRYING CAPACITY OF OVER 520 BOX CARS ! |

35

# THE ARK

(GEN. 6: 15)

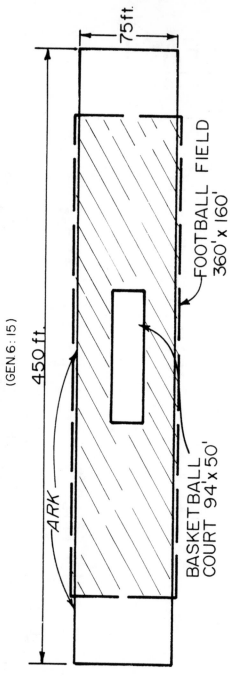

450 ft.

75 ft.

ARK

FOOTBALL FIELD
360' x 160'

BASKETBALL
COURT 94' x 50'

45 ft.

| | | |
|---|---|---|
| • HOW DID NOAH FEED AND KEEP THE ANIMALS? | | HIBERNATION A POSSIBLE SOLUTION |
| • WERE THERE DINOSAURS ON BOARD? YES! | A. | DRAWINGS OF BRONTOSAURUS HAVE BEEN FOUND ON WALLS OF RHODESIAN CAVES. |
| | B. | DINOSAUR AND HUMAN FOOTPRINTS HAVE BEEN FOUND IN THE SAME ROCK STRATA IN GLEN ROSE, TEXAS. |
| | C. | JOB SEEMS TO DESCRIBE A BRONTOSAURUS IN 40:15-24 |
| • HOW DID THE ANIMALS GET TO THEIR PRESENT LOCATION? | A. | BIOLOGISTS AGREE IN TIMES OF FLOOD LARGE MASSES OF LAND CAN BE SWEPT OUT TO SEA, CARRYING TREE AND ANIMALS |
| | B. | WITH FEW EXCEPTIONS, A DRY LAND PATH LEADS FROM MT. ARARAT TO ALL THE LANDS OF THE GLOBE. |
| • WHERE DID ALL THE FLOOD WATERS GO? | A. | IN GEN. 7:11 WE ARE INFORMED OF THE UPLIFT AND FRACTURING OF THE OCEAN FLOOR AT THE BEGINNING OF THE FLOOD. |
| | B. | IN GEN. 8:2-3 THE REVERSE PROCESS IS INDICATED, THAT IS, THE CREATION OF DEEP OCEAN BASINS TO RECEIVE MUCH OF THE FLOOD WATER |
| | C. | IN PSA. 104:8 THE AUTHOR STATES AT THE END OF THE FLOOD THAT THE MOUNTAINS ROSE AND THE VALLEYS SANK. |

| • HAS THE ARK BEEN SIGHTED SINCE IT LANDED ON MT. ARARAT | REPORTS PRIOR TO 1840 | REPORTS AFTER 1840 |
|---|---|---|
| | A. HERODOTUS<br>B. JOSEPHUS<br>C. THE KORAN<br>D. MARCO POLO | 1865 - HAJI YEARMAN<br>1893 - JOHN JOSEPH<br>1915 - W. ROSKOVITSKY<br>1917 - 150 RUSSIAN SOLDIERS<br>1933 - CARVETH WELLS<br>1941-45 - VARIOUS AIRMEN<br>1948 - RESIT<br>1943 - D. LIEDMAN<br>1953 - G. J. GREENE<br>- F. NAVARRA |

| SIMILAR EYEWITNESS REPORTS |
|---|
| A. A SHIP HALF-BURIED IN A LAKE 13,000 FEET HIGH |
| B. INSIDE ARK FILLED WITH WOODEN BAR SEPARATORS |
| C. OUTSIDE WOOD COVERED WITH HEAVY VARNISH SUBSTANCE |
| D. WOOD EXTREMELY HARD, ALMOST PETRIFIED |
| E. MAIN DOOR MISSING |

# GENESIS 9:20-27

| | |
|---|---|
| THE FAILURE OF NOAH: | DRUNKENNESS |
| THE SIN OF CANAAN: | UNKNOWN, PERHAPS THAT OF HOMOSEXUALITY |

## THE 3-FOLD PROPHECY OF NOAH

**CONCERNING HAM AND CANAAN:** "A SERVANT OF SERVANTS"

| GENERAL SERVITUDE TO SEED OF SHEM AND JAPHETH | *TECHNICAL PROFICIENCY* |
|---|---|
| • JOSHUA, DAVID AND SOLOMON SUBDUED THEM.<br>• ALEXANDER THE GREAT SUBDUED THEM.<br>• THE ROMANS SUBDUDED THEM. | THE FAMOUS CHRISTIAN ANTHROPOLOGIST *ARTHUR C. CUSTANCE* STATES THAT ALL THE EARLIEST CIVILIZATIONS OF NOTE WERE FOUNDED AND CARRIED TO THE HIGHEST TECHNICAL PROFICIENCY BY HAMETIC PEOPLES. |

**CONCERNING JAPHETH:** *"GOD SHALL ENLARGE JAPHETH, AND HE SHALL DWELL IN THE TENTS OF SHEM"*

| "GOD SHALL ENLARGE JAPHETH" | "AND HE SHALL DWELL IN THE TENTS OF SHEM" |
|---|---|
| • SINCE 539 B.C. WITH THE DEFEAT OF THE BABYLONIANS BY CYRUS THE GREAT, NO SEMITIC OR HAMITIC RACE HAS SUCCEEDED IN BREAKING THE WORLD SUPREMACY OF THE JAPHETHIC RACE. | THIS GLORIUS PROPHECY IS FULLY EXPLAINED BY PAUL IN ROM. 11:13-25 |

**CONCERNING SHEM:** *"BLESSED BE THE LORD GOD OF SHEM"*

• HERE IS OBVIOUSLY A REFERENCE TO THE SPECIAL FAVOR BESTOWED UPON SHEM'S DESCENDANTS, BEGINNING WITH ABRAHAM, AND ENDING IN A BETHLEHEM MANGER.

## THE 3-FOLD CONTRIBUTION OF NOAH'S SONS

| HAM | JAPHETH | SHEM |
|---|---|---|
| • TECHNICAL PROFICIENCY<br>• RESPONSIBLE FOR MAN'S PHYSICAL WELL-BEING. | • APPLICATION OF PHILOSOPHY<br>• DEVELOPMENT OF THE SCIENTIFIC METHOD.<br>• RESPONSIBLE FOR MAN'S MENTAL WELL-BEING. | • RELIGIOUS INSIGHTS<br>• RESPONSIBLE FOR MAN'S SPIRITUAL WELL-BEING. |

▲ THE ORIGIN OF FALSE RELIGION

▲ THE FIRST OF THREE ATTEMPTS TO CREATE A ONE-WORLD SYSTEM. (FOR THE OTHER TWO, SEE DAN. 2 AND REV. 13)

THE BEGINNING OF HUMAN LANGUAGE AND RACIAL DISTINCTIONS.

ARCHAEOLOGICAL EVIDENCE SUGGESTS THE TOWER WAS ACTUALLY A TEMPLE GIVEN OVER TO STAR WORSHIP.

THE TOWER PROBABLY INSTIGATED BY NIMROD, APOSTATE GRANDSON OF HAM (10:8-10).

# The Tower of BABEL

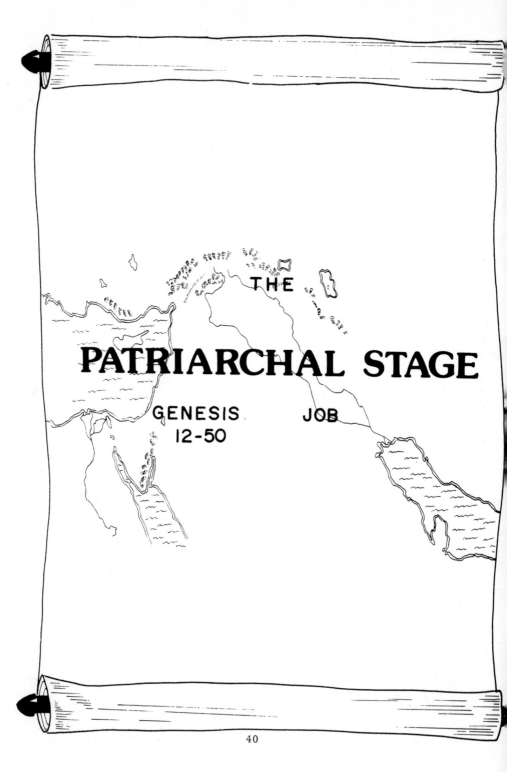

THE

# PATRIARCHAL STAGE

GENESIS      JOB
12-50

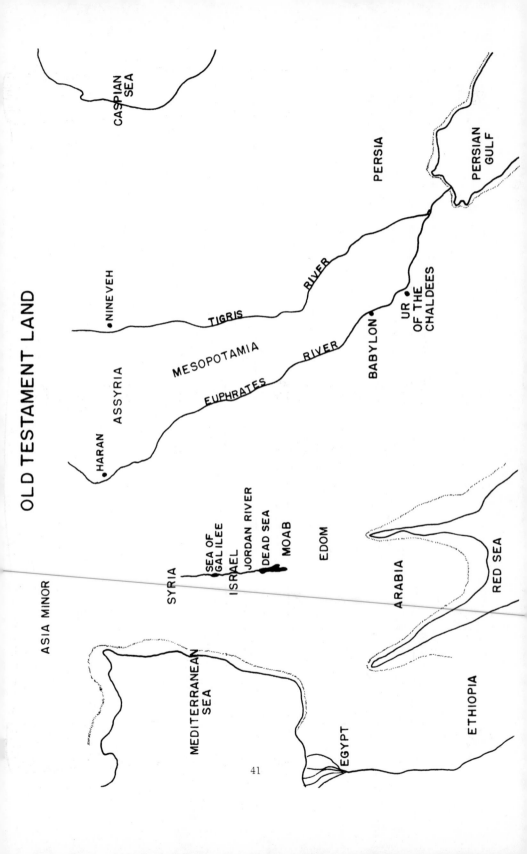

# Abraham

| | EVENT | DETAILS | REF. |
|---|---|---|---|
| I | CONVERSION AT UR <br>  TIGRIS, EUPHRATES, HARAN, UR | **SEVEN-FOLD PROMISE** <br> 1. I WILL MAKE OF THEE A GREAT NATION. <br> 2. I WILL BLESS THEE. <br> 3. I WILL MAKE THY NAME GREAT. <br> 4. THOU SHALT BE A BLESSING. <br> 5. I WILL BLESS THEM THAT BLESS THEE. <br> 6. I WILL CURSE HIM THAT CURSETH THEE. <br> 7. IN THEE SHALL ALL THE FAMILIES OF THE EARTH BE BLESSED. | Acts 7:2 <br> Gen. 11:31 <br> Gen. 12:1-4 <br> Josh. 24:3 |
| II | AT HARAN | **PARTIAL OBEDIENCE:** TAKES HIS FATHER AND SETTLES IN HARAN | Gen. 11:31, 32 |
| III | ARRIVES IN CANAAN | HE BUILDS AN ALTAR AND IS PROMISED THE LAND | Gen. 12:4, 9 |
| IV | HIS TRIP TO EGYPT <br> MED. SEA, CANAAN, DEAD SEA, EGYPT | ⬤ *REASON:* A FAMINE IN CANAAN <br> ⬤ *SIN:* DOUBT (Concerning GOD) AND DECEIT (Concerning SARAI) <br> ⬤ *TYPE:* EGYPT IS A TYPE OF THE WORLD <br> ⬤ *RESULTS:* 7 TRAGIC CONSEQUENCES: <br> 1. HE GRIEVED GOD <br> 2. HE WEAKENED HIS OWN FAITH <br> 3. HE WEAKENED THE FAITH OF SARAH <br> 4. HE BECAME A POOR TESTIMONY TO HIS NEPHEW LOT <br> 5. HE CAUSED THE PHARAOH TO BE AFFLICTED <br> 6. HE PICKS UP HAGAR THE EGYPTIAN HANDMAID <br> 7. HE PROVIDED A BAD EXAMPLE FOR HIS SON, ISAAC | Gen. 12:10-20 |

| | EVENT | DETAILS | REF |
|---|---|---|---|
| V | MEETS MELCHIZEDEK | ▲ BACKGROUND: ABRAM HAD WON A WAR AND RESCUED HIS NEPHEW<br>▲ IDENTITY OF MELCHIZEDEK: CHRIST? SHEM? UNKNOWN PRIEST?<br>▲ IMPORTANCE OF MEETING: FOUR FIRSTS RECORDED:<br>  1. FIRST COMMUNION (BREAD AND WINE)<br>  2. FIRST MENTION OF HOLY CITY (SALEM)<br>  3. FIRST MENTION OF PRIEST<br>  4. FIRST EXAMPLE OF TITHING | Gen. 13,14 |
| VI | RATIFICATION OF HIS COVENANT | ✸ BACKGROUND: THIS COVENANT WAS —<br>  1. ANNOUNCED IN GEN. 12:1-4<br>  2. CONFIRMED IN GEN. 13:14-17; 15:1-7<br>  3. RATIFIED IN GEN. 15:8-18<br>✸✸✸ METHOD EMPLOYED: A BLOOD AGREEMENT<br>✸✸✸ FEATURES: A LAND (*PALESTINE*) AND A PEOPLE (*ISRAEL*)<br>✸✸✸ TERMS: UNCONDITIONAL, NO STRINGS ATTACHED<br>✸✸ LANGUAGE: 3 KEY WORDS — *BELIEVED, COUNTED, RIGHTEOUSNESS*<br>✸ PROPHECY INVOLVED: THE 400 YEAR EGYPTIAN CAPTIVITY AND DELIVERENCE OF ISRAEL. | Gen. 15 |
| VII | HIS MARRIAGE TO HAGAR | ● THE PLAN OF SARAI<br>● THE PLIGHT OF HAGAR<br>● THE AID OF AN ANGEL<br>● THE BIRTH OF ISHMAEL | GEN. 16 |
| VIII | ABRAM AT 99 | ▲ SOME NEW NAMES<br>  1. ABRAM CHANGED TO ABRAHAM (FATHER OF NATIONS)<br>  2. SARAI CHANGED TO SARAH (A PRINCESS)<br>  3. GOD INTRODUCED AS EL SHADDAI (THE FRUITFUL ONE)<br>▲ A NEW SEAL: CIRCUMCISION NOW BECOMES THE SIGN OF GOD'S COVENANT. | GEN. 17 |

| EVENT | | DETAILS | REF. |
|---|---|---|---|
| **IX** | GOOD NEWS & BAD NEWS | ● **ABRAHAM** IS VISITED BY THE **LORD** AND TWO ANGELS | GEN. 18,19 |
| | | THE **GOOD NEWS**: HIS LONG PROMISED HEIR WOULD BE BORN NEXT SPRING. | |
| | | ● THE **BAD NEWS**: **GOD** PLANNED TO DESTROY **SODOM**, LOT'S HOME CITY. | |
| | | ● **ABRAHAM** PRAYS FOR THE DOOMED CITY. | |
| | | ● **SODOM** IS DESTROYED. ONLY LOT AND HIS TWO DAUGHTERS SURVIVE. | |
| **X** | ABRAHAM IN PHILISTIA | ▲ DURING A FAMINE HE AGAIN LEAVES CANAAN AND LIES ABOUT SARAH. | GEN. 20 |
| **XI** | THE HEIR OF THE COVENANT | ▲ ISAAC IS BORN | GEN. 21 |
| | | ▲ HAGAR AND ISHMAEL ARE SENT AWAY | |
| **XII** | FORESHADOWS OF CALVARY | ● THE **TYPE**: 1. SACRIFICE OF ISAAC 2. SUBSTITUTE FOR ISAAC | GEN. 22 |
| | | ● THE **LOCATION**: MT. MORIAH, THOUGHT TO BE GOLGOTHA | |
| | | ● THE **REVELATION**: A NEW NAME FOR **GOD, JEHOVAH - JIREH** *(THE LORD WILL PROVIDE)* | |
| **XIII** | DEATH OF SARAH | SARAH DIES AT 127 AND IS BURIED IN THE CAVE OF MACHPELAH | GEN. 23 |
| **XIV** | COMMANDING HIS SERVANT | ▲ **ABRAHAM'S COMMAND**: TO FETCH A BRIDE FOR ISAAC. | GEN. 24 |
| | | ▲ **THE SERVANT'S PRAYER**: SHOW ME THE RIGHT GIRL. | |
| | | ▲ **THE LORD'S ANSWER**: REBEKAH IS THE ONE. | |
| | | ▲ **THE SCRIPTURAL TYPES**: THIS IS THE MOST TYPE FILLED CHAPTER IN THE BIBLE. | |
| | | 1. ABRAHAM IS A TYPE OF THE FATHER | |
| | | 2. ISAAC IS A TYPE OF THE SON | |
| | | 3. THE SERVANT IS A TYPE OF THE HOLY SPIRIT | |
| | | 4. REBEKAH IS A TYPE OF THE CHURCH | |

| | EVENT | DETAILS | REF. |
|---|---|---|---|
| **XV** | HIS MARRIAGE TO KETURAH | ✦ SHE BORE HIM SIX SONS<br><br>✦ THE 4th WAS MIDIAN, FATHER OF THE MIDIANITES | GEN. 25: 1-6 |
| **XVI** | HIS DEATH | ● AGE: 175<br><br>● PLACE OF BURIAL: THE CAVE OF MACHPELAH<br><br>● EPITATH:<br><br>HEB. 11: 8-10<br><br>"8 BY FAITH ABRAHAM, WHEN HE WAS CALLED TO GO OUT INTO A PLACE WHICH HE SHOULD AFTER RECEIVE FOR AN INHERITANCE, OBEYED; AND HE WENT OUT, NOT KNOWING WHITHER HE WENT.<br><br>9 BY FAITH HE SOJOURNED IN THE LAND OF PROMISE, AS IN A STRANGE COUNTRY, DWELLING IN TABERNACLES WITH ISAAC AND JACOB, THE HEIRS WITH HIM OF THE SAME PROMISE:<br><br>10 FOR HE LOOKED FOR A CITY WHICH HATH FOUNDATIONS, WHOSE BUILDER AND MAKER IS GOD."<br><br> | GEN. 25: 7-10,<br><br>HEB. 11: 8-10 |

# IMPORTANT PLACES IN THE STORY OF ABRAHAM

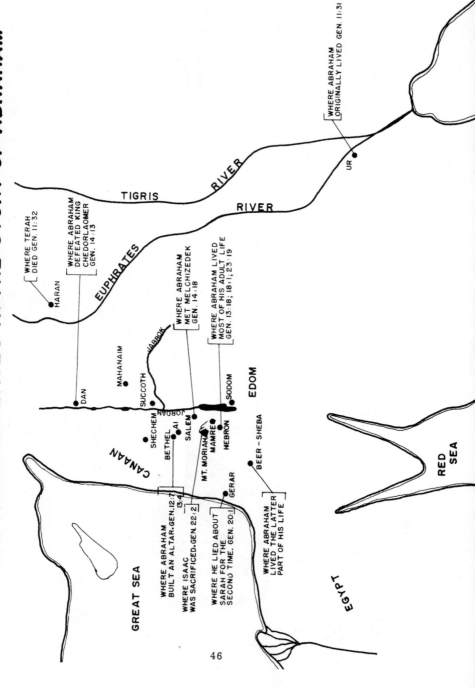

WHERE ABRAHAM ORIGINALLY LIVED GEN. 11:31

UR

TIGRIS RIVER

RIVER

EUPHRATES

WHERE TERAH DIED GEN. 11:32

WHERE ABRAHAM DEFEATED KING CHEDORLAOMER GEN. 14:13

HARAN

JABBOK

MAHANAIM

DAN

SUCCOTH

WHERE ABRAHAM MET MELCHIZEDEK GEN. 14:18

WHERE ABRAHAM LIVED MOST OF HIS ADULT LIFE GEN. 13:18; 18:1; 23:19

SHECHEM

BETHEL

AI

SALEM

JORDAN

MT. MORIAH

MAMRE

HEBRON

SODOM

EDOM

CANAAN

GREAT SEA

WHERE ABRAHAM BUILT AN ALTAR. GEN. 12:7; 13:4

WHERE ISAAC WAS SACRIFICED. GEN. 22:2

WHERE HE LIED ABOUT SARAH FOR THE SECOND TIME. GEN. 20:1

GERAR

BEER-SHEBA

WHERE ABRAHAM LIVED THE LATTER PART OF HIS LIFE

EGYPT

RED SEA

# ISAAC

### The Submissive Son — GEN. 22:1-4

★ HE IS OFFERED UP BY HIS FATHER ABRAHAM

### THE GENTLE GROOM — GEN. 24:62-67

★ HE MEETS REBEKAH FOR THE FIRST TIME

### The Praying Parent — GEN. 25:19-26

★ HE PRAYS THAT GOD WOULD BLESS THEM WITH CHILDREN

★ REBEKAH GIVES BIRTH TO TWINS — ESAU & JACOB

### THE COPY CAT — GEN. 26:1-11

★ LIKE HIS FATHER HE LEAVES PALESTINE DURING A FAMINE

★ LIKE HIS FATHER HE LIES ABOUT HIS WIFE

47

## The Willing Worker
GEN. 26:17-33

✴ SOME JEALOUS PHILISTINES HAD FILLED UP ABRAHAM'S WELLS WITH DEBRIS.

✴ ISAAC REDIGS AND CLEANS OUT THOSE WELLS.

## THE FRUSTRATED FATHER
GEN. 27:1-45

✴ AT 137 ISAAC FEELS HIS DEATH IS NEAR.

✴ ESAU IS INSTRUCTED TO PREPARE HIM A MEAL AND RECEIVE THE PATRIARCHAL BLESSING

✴ REBEKAH ARRANGES TO DECEIVE THE DIM-EYED ISAAC BY SUBSTITUTING JACOB.

✴ JACOB RECEIVES THE BLESSING INTENDED FOR ESAU.

✴ ISAAC SENDS JACOB AWAY THAT HIS SON MIGHT ESCAPE ESAU'S REVENGE

48

# LIFE OF JACOB

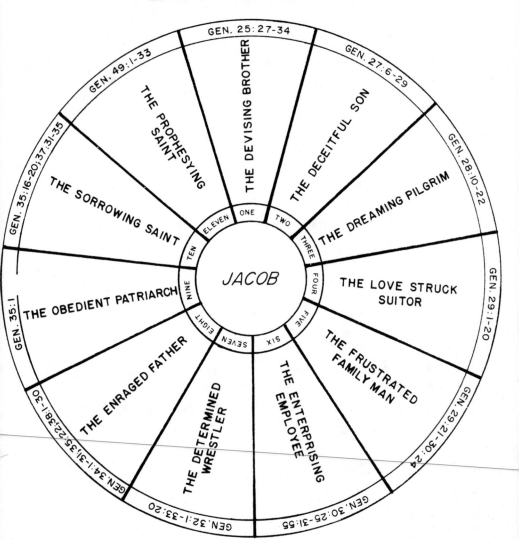

GEN. 25:27-34

GEN. 49:1-33

GEN. 27:6-29

THE PROPHESYING SAINT

THE DEVISING BROTHER

THE DECEITFUL SON

GEN. 35:16-20;37:31-35

GEN. 28:10-22

THE SORROWING SAINT

THE DREAMING PILGRIM

ELEVEN   ONE   TWO

TEN                    THREE

JACOB

NINE                    FOUR

THE LOVE STRUCK SUITOR

THE OBEDIENT PATRIARCH

EIGHT   SEVEN   SIX   FIVE

GEN. 35:1

GEN. 29:1-20

THE ENRAGED FATHER

THE DETERMINED WRESTLER

THE ENTERPRISING EMPLOYEE

THE FRUSTRATED FAMILY MAN

GEN. 34:1-31;35:22;38:1-30

GEN. 32:1-33:20

GEN. 30:25-31:55

GEN. 29:21-30:24

49

THE
DEVISING
BROTHER

GEN. 25:27-34

▼ HE PRESSURES ESAU INTO TRADING TO HIM THE BIRTH RIGHT.

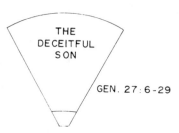

THE
DECEITFUL
SON

GEN. 27:6-29

▼ HE TRICKS HIS FATHER TO GIVE HIM THE BLESSING.

THE
DREAMING
PILGRIM

GEN. 28:10-22

▼ HE SEES A LADDER SET UP FROM EARTH TO HEAVEN AT BETHEL
▼ ANGELS WERE ASCENDING AND DESCENDING UPON IT.
▼ GOD CONFIRMS TO HIM THE ABRAHAMIC COVENANT.
▼ UPON AWAKENING HE ANOINTED A ROCK PILE AND VOWED TO
SERVE GOD.

THE
LOVE
STRUCK
SUITOR

GEN. 29: 1-20

▼ HE MEETS RACHEL HIS COUSIN AND FUTURE WIFE BESIDE A WELL.
▼ HERE BEGINS ONE OF HISTORY'S GREAT LOVE STORIES.
▼ HE PROMISES RACHEL'S FATHER LABAN (JACOB'S UNCLE AND
FUTURE FATHER-IN-LAW) TO WORK 7 YEARS FOR HER HAND
IN MARRIAGE.

50

THE
FRUSTRATED
FAMILY
MAN

GEN. 29:21-30:24

▼ HE IS DECEIVED ON HIS WEDDING NIGHT BY LABAN WHO SECRETLY
  SUBSTITUTED LEAH (RACHEL'S OLDEST SISTER) FOR RACHEL.

▼ JACOB IS FURIOUS BUT AGREES TO WORK YET ANOTHER 7 YEARS
  FOR RACHEL.

▼ HE NOW HAS TWO WIVES AND WOULD GATHER YET ANOTHER TWO,
  FOR BOTH RACHEL AND LEAH PRESENT TO HIM THEIR PERSONAL
  HANDMAIDS FOR CHILDBEARING PURPOSES.

  THESE FOUR WOMEN WOULD BEAR JACOB 12 SONS AND 1 DAUGHTER.

| WIFE | *LEAH* | *BILAH* | *ZILPAH* | *RACHEL* |
|------|--------|---------|----------|----------|
| SON | 1. REUBEN<br>2. SIMEON<br>3. LEVI<br>4. JUDAH<br><br><br>9. ISSACHAR<br>10. ZEBULON | (RACHEL'S HANDMAID)<br><br><br>5. DAN<br>6. NAPHTALI | (LEAH'S HANDMAID)<br><br><br><br>7. GAD<br>8. ASHER | <br><br><br><br><br><br>11. JOSEPH<br>12. BENJAMIN |
| DAUGHTER | DINAH | | | |

THE
ENTERPRISING
EMPLOYEE

GEN. 30:25-31:55

▼ JACOB GOES IN BUSINESS WITH LABAN AND BECOMES A WEALTHY MAN.

▼ UPON BEING ORDERED BY GOD TO RETURN HOME, HE BREAKS CAMP
  WITHOUT TELLING LABAN.

▼ LABAN CHASES HIM DOWN AND ACCUSES JACOB (AMONG OTHER THINGS)
  OF STEALING HIS HOUSEHOLD GODS.

▼ LABAN AND JACOB COME TO A TRUCE AND BUILD A MEMORIAL PILE
  OF STONES.

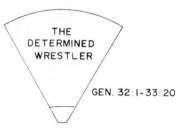

THE
DETERMINED
WRESTLER

GEN. 32:1-33:20

▼ *JACOB LEARNS THAT ESAU WAS ON HIS WAY TO MEET HIM RIDING WITH 400 MEN.*

▼ *FILLED WITH FEAR JACOB WRESTLES WITH GOD IN PRAYER ALL NIGHT LONG BY THE BROOK JABBOK.*

▼ *HE IS REASSURED BY GOD FOR THIS AND HIS NAME IS CHANGED FROM JACOB TO ISRAEL.*

▼ *THE FOLLOWING MEETING BETWEEN ISRAEL AND ESAU WAS VERY FRIENDLY.*

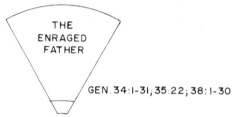

THE
ENRAGED
FATHER

GEN. 34:1-31; 35:22; 38:1-30

▼ *OVER THE SIN OF MURDER, COMMITTED BY LEVI AND SIMEON*

1. THESE BOYS TRICKED A GROUP OF DESERT MEN WHOSE LEADER HAD SEDUCED DINAH, THEIR SISTER, INTO CIRCUMCISING THEMSELVES.

2. ON THE THIRD DAY WHEN THEY WERE HELPLESS TO DEFEND THEMSELVES BECAUSE OF THEIR SELF-INFLICTED WOUNDS, JACOB'S TWO SONS SLAUGHTERED THEM LIKE ANIMALS.

▼ *OVER THE SIN OF ADULTERY, COMMITTED BY REUBEN.*

"AND IT CAME TO PASS, WHEN ISRAEL DWELT IN THAT LAND, THAT REUBEN WENT AND LAY WITH BILHAH, HIS FATHER'S CONCUBINE: AND ISRAEL HEARD IT..." (GEN. 35:22)

▼ *OVER THE SIN OF ADULTERY, COMMITTED BY JUDAH.*

1. TO SEEK REVENGE UPON JUDAH (FOR REFUSING A REQUEST OF HERS) TAMAR, HIS DAUGHTER-IN-LAW DISGUISES HERSELF AS A COMMON HARLOT AND INTICES HIM INTO HER TENT FOR SEXUAL PURPOSES.

2. TAMAR BECOMES PREGNANT AND JUDAH ORDERS HER DEATH FOR IMMORALITY UNTIL HE LEARNS WHO THE FATHER OF THE CHILD REALLY WAS!

THE
OBEDIENT
PATRIARCH

GEN. 35:1-15

- JACOB IS ORDERED BY GOD BACK TO BETHEL.
- IN PREPARATION FOR THIS TRIP JACOB INSTRUCTS HIS HOUSEHOLD
  TO DESTROY THEIR IDOLS AND PREPARE THEIR HEARTS.
- HE BUILDS AN ALTAR AT BETHEL AND CALLS IT EL-BETHEL-
  THE GOD OF THE HOUSE OF GOD.

THE
SORROWING
SAINT

GEN. 35:16-20; 37:31-35

- HE LOSES HIS BELOVED WIFE RACHEL IN CHILDBEARING.
- HE BURIES HIS FATHER ISAAC.
- HE IS LED TO BELIEVE THAT JOSEPH HAS BEEN KILLED AND EATEN
  BY A WILD BEAST.

THE
PROPHESYING
SAINT

GEN. 49:1-33

- UPON DISCOVERING THE REAL TRUTH ABOUT JOSEPH, JACOB MOVES
  HIS ENTIRE FAMILY TO EGYPT.
- AT AGE 147 HE REALIZES DEATH IS NEAR AND BESTOWS THE
  FOLLOWING BLESSINGS AND PROPHECIES.

# THE LIFE OF JOSEPH

## THE FAVORED SON (GEN. 37)

**THE DREAMS OF JOSEPH** — IN TWO SEPARATE DREAMS JOSEPH SEES HIMSELF OCCUPYING A PLACE OF GREAT IMPORTANCE.

**THE DECEIT OF HIS BROTHERS** — HE IS SOLD INTO EGYPTIAN SLAVERY BY HIS OWN BROTHERS.

**THE DESPAIR OF HIS FATHER** — JOSEPH'S BROTHERS STAIN HIS COAT WITH THE BLOOD OF A KID AND ALLOW THEIR FATHER TO CONCLUDE A WILD BEAST HAD EATEN HIM.

## THE FAITHFUL STEWARD (GEN. 39)

**HIS SERVICE** — HE SERVES FAITHFULLY IN THE HOME OF AN EGYPTIAN ARMY OFFICER.

**HIS SELF-CONTROL** — HE REFUSES THE SEXUAL ADVANCES OF THE ARMY OFFICER'S WIFE.

**HIS SUFFERINGS** — JOSEPH IS FALSELY ACCUSED OF RAPE AND THROWN INTO PRISON.

## THE FORGOTTEN SERVANT (GEN. 40)

**THE REVELATION BY JOSEPH** — JOSEPH FINDS HIMSELF IN THE SAME CELL WITH THE PHARAOH'S BUTLER AND BAKER WHO WERE ALSO IMPRISONED.

THESE TWO MEN EXPERIENCE STRANGE DREAMS. JOSEPH INTERPRETS THAT WITHIN THREE DAYS THE KING WOULD FREE THE BUTLER BUT EXECUTE THE BAKER.

**THE ELEVATION OF JOSEPH** — ALL THIS COMES TRUE. HOWEVER, UPON HIS RELEASE THE BUTLER FORGETS ALL ABOUT JOSEPH.

## THE FAMED STATESMAN (GEN. 41-44)

**THE REVELATION BY JOSEPH** — SEVERAL YEARS LATER THE PHARAOH EXPERIENCES TWO STRANGE DREAMS, BUT NO ONE COULD INTERPRET THEM.

THE BUTLER REMEMBERS JOSEPH. HE IS RELEASED AND INTERPRETS THE DREAMS AS A PROPHECY OF A COMING 7-YEAR HARVEST CROP, FOLLOWED BY 7 YEARS OF FAMINE.

**THE ELEVATION OF JOSEPH** — JOSEPH IS PROMOTED ON THE SPOT BY THE PHARAOH TO EGYPT'S HIGHEST OFFICE - THAT OF FOOD ADMINISTRATOR.

**THE FRUSTRATION OF JOSEPH'S BROTHERS** — HIS BROTHERS ARRIVE IN EGYPT TO BUY FOOD. HE RECOGNIZES THEM BUT THEY DO NOT KNOW HIM.

HE PRETENDS TO BE HARSH, EVEN THREATENING TO IMPRISON BENJAMIN ON A THEFT CHARGE.

| THE FORGIVING SAINT (GEN. 45-48) | THE FRUITFUL SHADE TREE (GEN. 49-50) |
|---|---|
| **JOSEPH AND HIS BROTHERS** — UNABLE TO HIDE HIS IDENTITY ANY LONGER, JOSEPH REVEALS HIMSELF TO HIS BROTHERS. | **HE RECEIVES HIS FATHER'S BLESSING** — *"JOSEPH IS A FRUITFUL BOUGH... BY A WELL, WHOSE BRANCHES RUN OVER THE WALL....HIS HANDS WERE MADE STRONG BY....THE MIGHTY GOD... ...THE ALMIGHTY... SHALL BLESS THEE WITH THE BLESSINGS OF HEAVEN ABOVE..."* (GEN. 49:22-25) |
| **JOSEPH AND HIS FATHER** — THE OLD PATRIARCH JACOB IS PERSUADED TO COME TO EGYPT AND LIVE WITH JOSEPH. | **HE RETURNS HIS FATHER'S BODY** — JACOB'S EMBALMED BODY IS CARRIED BACK TO PALESTINE BY JOSEPH AND BURIED IN THE CAVE OF MACHPELAH. |
| **JOSEPH AND HIS SONS** — JOSEPH'S TWO SONS, EPHRAIM AND MANASSEH ARE BLESSED BY THEIR GRANDFATHER JACOB. SEE ALSO HEB. 11:21 | |

## THE FORESHADOW OF THE SAVIOUR

| JOSEPH | NOTE THE AMAZING SIMILARITIES BETWEEN THESE TWO | JESUS |
|---|---|---|
| GEN. 37:3 | • Beloved By Their FATHERS | MAT. 3:17 |
| 37:2 | • Regarded Themselves as SHEPHERDS | JN. 10:11-14 |
| 37:13-14 | • Sent By Their FATHERS To Their BRETHREN | LK. 20:13, HEB. 2:12 |
| 37:4,5,8 | • Hated By Their Brethren Without A Cause | JN. 1:11; 7:5; 15:25 |
| 37:20 | • Plotted Against By Their Brethren | JN. 11:53 |
| 39:7 | • SEVERELY TEMPTED | MAT. 4:1 |
| 37:26 | • TAKEN TO EGYPT | MAT. 2:14-15 |
| 37:23 | • Stripped of Their Robes | JN. 19:23-24 |
| 37:28 | • Sold for the Price of a Slave | MAT. 26:15 |
| 39:20 | • BOUND | MAT. 27:2 |
| 39:20 | • Remained Silent and Offered No Defense | ISA. 53:7 |
| 39:16-18 | • FALSELY ACCUSED | MAT. 26:59-60 |
| 39:2,21,23 | • Experienced GOD'S Presence Through Everything | JN. 16:32 |
| 39:21 | • Respected By Their Jailors | LK. 23:47 |
| 40:2-3 | • Placed with Two Prisoners, One of Which was Later Lost, the Other Saved | LK. 23:32 |
| 41:46 | • Both Around 30 at the Beginning of Their Ministry | LK. 3:23 |
| 41:41 | • Both Highly Exalted After Their Sufferings | PHIL. 2:9-11 |
| 41:45 | • Both Took Non-Jewish Brides | EPH. 3:1-12 |
| 42:7-8 | • Both Lost to Their Brethren for Awhile | ROM. 10:1-3, 11:7-8 |
| 45:1-15 | • Both Forgave and Restored Their Repentent Brothers | ZECH. 12:10-12 |
| 41:57 | • Both Visited and Honored By All Earthly NATIONS | ISA. 2:2-3; 49:6 |

IMPORTANT PLACES IN THE STORY OF *JACOB, ISAAC, AND JOSEPH*

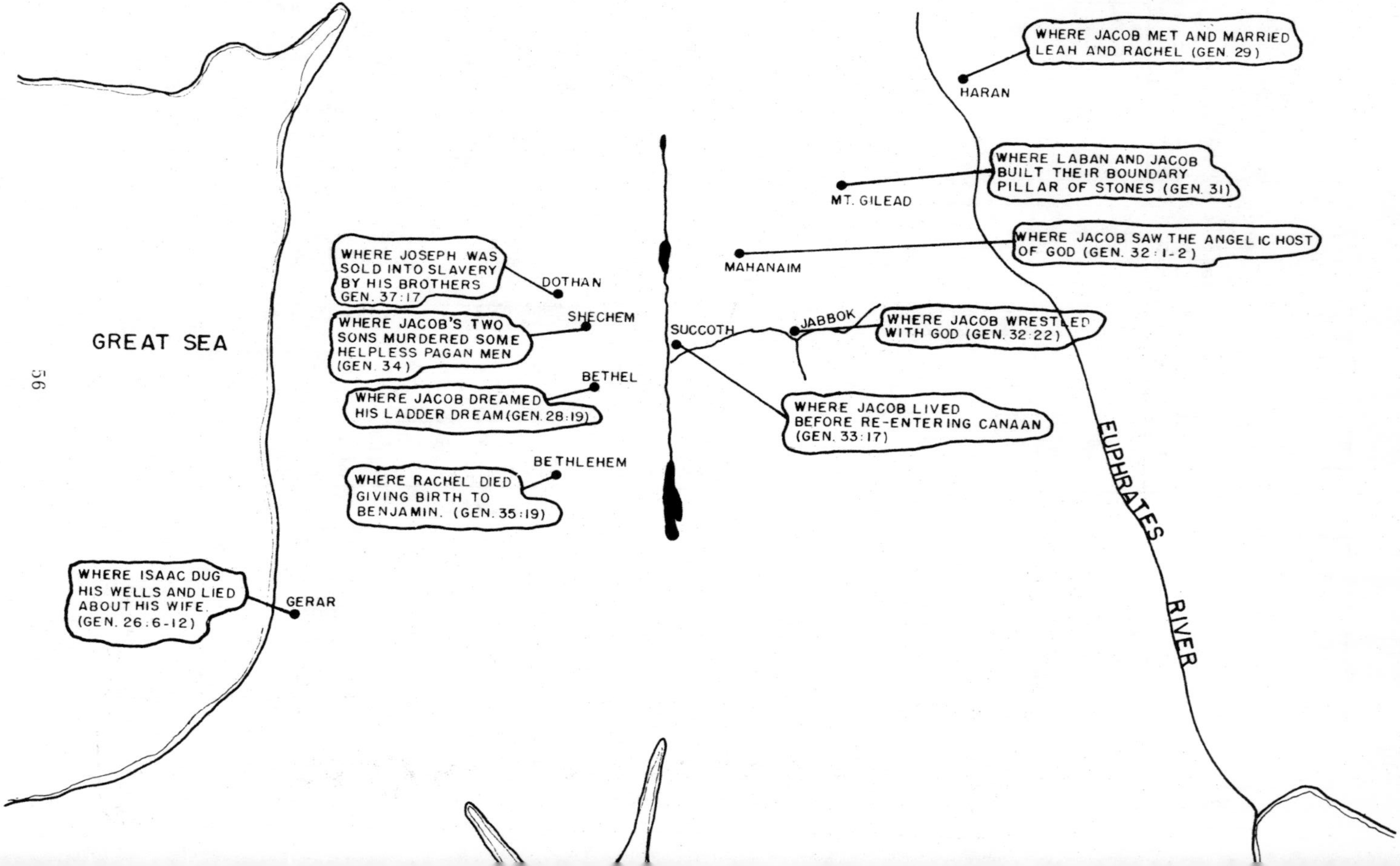

WHERE JACOB MET AND MARRIED LEAH AND RACHEL (GEN. 29)

WHERE LABAN AND JACOB BUILT THEIR BOUNDARY PILLAR OF STONES (GEN. 31)

WHERE JACOB SAW THE ANGELIC HOST OF GOD (GEN. 32:1-2)

WHERE JACOB WRESTLED WITH GOD (GEN. 32:22)

WHERE JACOB LIVED BEFORE RE-ENTERING CANAAN (GEN. 33:17)

EUPHRATES RIVER

HARAN

MT. GILEAD

MAHANAIM

JABBOK

SUCCOTH

WHERE JOSEPH WAS SOLD INTO SLAVERY BY HIS BROTHERS (GEN. 37:17)

WHERE JACOB'S TWO SONS MURDERED SOME HELPLESS PAGAN MEN (GEN. 34)

WHERE JACOB DREAMED HIS LADDER DREAM (GEN. 28:19)

WHERE RACHEL DIED GIVING BIRTH TO BENJAMIN. (GEN. 35:19)

DOTHAN

SHECHEM

BETHEL

BETHLEHEM

GREAT SEA

GERAR

WHERE ISAAC DUG HIS WELLS AND LIED ABOUT HIS WIFE (GEN. 26:6-12)

56

THE BOOK OF JOB

HIS TERRIBLE TRIALS

HIS WHIMPERING WIFE

HIS FICKLE FRIENDS

HIS DOUBTS AND DEFENCES

HIS GLORIOUS GOD

HIS BOUNTIFUL BLESSINGS

# HIS TERRIBLE TRIALS

### NATURE OF TRIALS  (1-2 )

1. OXEN AND DONKEYS STOLEN AND FARMHANDS KILLED.

2. SHEEP AND HERDSMEN BURNED BY FIRE

3. CAMELS ARE STOLEN AND SERVANTS KILLED.

4. SONS AND DAUGHTERS DIE IN A MIGHTY WIND.

5. JOB HIMSELF IS STRUCK WITH BOILS.

### BACKGROUND OF TRIALS

Job's motives for worshipping GOD had been challenged by Satan during a confrontation in the heavenlies.

A Sovereign God thereupon allows the five trials.

## HIS WHIMPERING WIFE

*"Then said his wife unto him, Dost thou still retain thine integrity ? Curse GOD, and die." (2:9)*

# HIS FICKLE FRIENDS

| NAME | SERMON LOCATION | SERMON AUTHORITY | SERMON CONCLUSION |
|---|---|---|---|
| ELIPHAZ | 4, 5, 15, 22 | PERSONAL EXPERIENCE 4:8, 12-16 | "YOU ARE SUFFERING BECAUSE OF YOUR SIN!" (4:7,8;15:6)<br>1.YOU HAVE CHEATED THE POOR (22:6)<br>2.YOU HAVE NOT FED THE HUNGRY (22:7)<br>3.YOU HAVE MISTREATED WIDOWS AND ORPHANS (22:9)<br>4.YOU ARE A WINDBAG! (15:2)<br>"MY ADVICE: REPENT AND TURN BACK TO GOD!' (22:21-28) |
| BILDAD | 8, 18, 25 | TRADITION 8: 8-10 | "YOU ARE SUFFERING BECAUSE OF YOUR SIN!" (8:20)<br>"MY ADVICE: REPENT AND TURN BACK TO GOD!" (8:5-6) |
| ZOPHAR | 11, 20 | DOGMATISM 11:6; 20:4 | "YOU ARE SUFFERING BECAUSE OF YOUR SIN!" (11:4-6; 20:4-5)<br>"MY ADVICE: REPENT AND TURN BACK TO GOD!" (11:13-15) |
| ELIHU | 32-37 | ELIHU THOUGHT HE WAS GOD'S ANSWER TO JOB'S PROBLEM 33:6 | 1.YOU ARE GUILTY OF FOOLISH SPEAKING (34:35-37;36:16)<br>2.YOU ARE GUILTY OF FALSE RIGHTEOUSNESS (35:2)<br>3.CONSIDER GOD'S GLORY AND GREATNESS (37:14-24) |

# HIS DEFENSES AND DIALOGUES

## THE SUFFERING PATRIARCH RESPONDS TO HIS ACCUSERS IN 9 SEPARATE SPEECHES

| ONE | CHAPTER 3 | FOUR | 12,13,14 | SEVEN | 21 |
|---|---|---|---|---|---|
| TWO | 6 - 7 | FIVE | 16,17 | EIGHT | 23,24 |
| THREE | 9 - 10 | SIX | 19 | NINE | 26-31 |

*DURING THESE 9 SPEECHES JOB DISCUSSES 14 TOPICS. THESE ARE :*

1. I AM RIGHTEOUS AND THEREFORE NOT SUFFERING FOR MY SIN. (27:6; 31:1-40)
2. IN THE PAST I HAVE PERFORMED MANY GOOD WORKS. (29:12-17; 30:25)
3. OH, FOR THOSE GOOD OLD DAYS WHEN I ENJOYED HEALTH, WEALTH AND RESPECT. (29:1-11, 20-25)
4. BUT NOW I AM BEING UNFAIRLY PUNISHED BY GOD. (9:16,17,30,31,32,33; 13:26,27; 10:2,7, 8, 19:6-11; 30:20,21)
5. MY THREE SO-CALLED FRIENDS ARE MISERABLE COMFORTERS (12:2; 13:4; 16:2; 19:3)
6. IF THEY WERE IN MY PLACE I WOULD HELP THEM AND NOT UNJUSTLY ACCUSE THEM (16:4,5)
7. EVEN MY NEIGHBORS, ASSOCIATES AND SERVANTS HAVE TURNED AGAINST ME. (19:13-22; 30:1,9,10)
8. I WISH I COULD FIND THE ANSWERS FOR ALL THIS. (28:12-28)
9. I WISH I COULD FIND GOD. (23:8,9)
10. MY FLESH IS CLOTHED WITH WORMS. (7:5,13,14; 30:17,18,30)
11. I WISH I HAD NEVER BEEN BORN. (3:3-11,16; 10:18)
12. I WISH I WERE DEAD. (6:8,9; 7:15,16)
13. I HAVE NO HOPE. (10:20-22)
14. IN SPITE OF ALL, I'LL TRUST GOD. (13:15; 16:19; 23:10)

# HIS GLORIOUS GOD

SUDDENLY FROM OUT OF A WHIRLWIND COMES THE MIGHTY VOICE OF GOD. THE SULLEN JOB IS THEN SUBJECTED TO A 60-QUESTION QUIZ. NOTE SOME OF THEM:

## GOD'S FIRST SERIES OF QUESTIONS: JOB 38-39

1. **JOB 38:4**
   "WHERE WAST THOU WHEN I LAID THE FOUNDATIONS OF THE EARTH? DECLARE, IF THOU HAST UNDERSTANDING."

2. **JOB 38:18**
   "HAST THOU PERCEIVED THE BREADTH OF THE EARTH? DECLARE IF THOU KNOWEST IT ALL."

3. **JOB 38:19**
   "WHERE IS THE WAY WHERE LIGHT DWELLETH? AND AS FOR DARKNESS, WHERE IS THE PLACE THEREOF."

4. **JOB 38:24**
   "BY WHAT WAY IS THE LIGHT PARTED, WHICH SCATTERETH THE EAST WIND UPON THE EARTH?"

5. **JOB 38:28**
   "HATH THE RAIN A FATHER? OR WHO HATH BEGOTTEN THE DROPS OF DEW?"

6. **JOB 40:2**
   "SHALL HE THAT CONTENDETH WITH THE ALMIGHTY INSTRUCT HIM? HE THAT REPROVETH GOD, LET HIM ANSWER IT."

### JOB'S REPLY: 4:4-5

## GOD'S SECOND SERIES OF QUESTIONS: JOB 40:6-41:33

1. **JOB 40:15**
   "BEHOLD NOW THE BEHEMOTH, WHICH I MADE WITH THEE; HE EATETH GRASS AS AN OX."

2. **JOB 41:1**
   "CANST THOU DRAW OUT LEVIATHAN WITH AN HOOK? OR HIS TONGUE WITH A CORD WHICH THOU LETTEST DOWN?"

   *NOTE:* THESE TWO CREATURES MAY VERY WELL REFER TO A LAND DINOSAUR AND A SEA DINOSAUR!

### JOB'S REPLY: 42:1-5

# HIS BOUNTIFUL BLESSINGS

JOB 42:7-17

| | JOB HAS BEEN SUBJECTED TO FIVE FIERY TRIALS AND HAS PARTICIPATED IN FIVE PAINFUL DEBATES, BUT NOW HE RECEIVES AT THE HAND OF GOD A TEN-FOLD BLESSING! |
|---|---|
| 1. | HE IS ALLOWED TO SEE THE GLORY OF GOD. |
| 2. | HE SEES HIMSELF AS GOD SEES HIM. (THIS IS ALWAYS A BLESSING) |
| 3. | HE IS VINDICATED BY GOD BEFORE THE EYES OF HIS THREE CRITICAL FRIENDS. |
| 4. | HE DISCOVERS THE JOY OF PRAYING FOR THESE THREE FRIENDS. |
| 5. | HIS FORMER HEALTH IS FULLY RESTORED. |
| 6. | HE IS COMFORTED BY HIS BROTHERS AND SISTER. |
| 7. | HE IS GIVEN MONEY SHOWER AND DOUBLE HIS FORMER WEALTH. |
| 8. | HE IS GIVEN SEVEN MORE SONS AND THREE MORE DAUGHTERS. |
| 9. | HE LIVES TO ENJOY HIS GRANDCHILDREN AND GREAT-GRANDCHILDREN. |
| 10. | HE IS GIVEN AN ADDITIONAL 140 YEARS --- TWICE THE NUMBER NORMALLY ACCORDED A MAN. SEE PSALMS 90:10. |

## SOME REASONS FOR JOB'S SUFFERINGS

1. THAT SATAN MIGHT BE SILENCED (1:9-11; 2:4-5).
2. THAT JOB MIGHT SEE GOD (42:5).
3. THAT JOB MIGHT SEE HIMSELF (40:4; 42:6).
4. THAT JOB'S FRIENDS MIGHT LEARN NOT TO JUDGE (42:7).
5. THAT JOB MIGHT LEARN TO PRAY FOR, RATHER THAN TO LASH OUT AGAINST HIS CRITICS (42:10).
6. TO DEMONSTRATE THAT ALL GOD'S PLANS FOR HIS OWN EVENTUALLY HAVE HAPPY ENDINGS (42:10)!

# CLASSIC STATEMENTS IN JOB

1. "He taketh the wise in their own craftiness . . ." (5:13). Quoted by Paul in I Corinthians 3:19.

2. "Behold, happy is the man whom God correcteth; therefore, despise not thou the chastening of the Almighty" (5:17). Quoted in Hebrews 12:5-6.

3. "Neither is there any daysman between us that might lay his hand upon us both" (9:33). The word daysman, refers to a mediator. In the New Testament, of course, all this would change. See I Timothy 2:5.

4. "Man that is born of a woman is of few days, and full of trouble. He cometh forth like a flower, and is cut down; he fleeth also as a shadow, and continueth not" (14:1-2).

5. "They have gaped upon me with their mouth; they have smitten me upon the cheek reproachfully; they have gathered themselves together against me. God hath delivered me to the ungodly, and turned me over into the hands of the wicked" (16:10,11).

   These words are repeated (in paraphrase fashion) in Psalms 22:13; 35:21, which Psalms refer to the sufferings of Christ on the cross.

6. "Also now, behold, my witness is in heaven, and my record is on high" (16:19).

7. "But he knoweth the way that I take; when he hath tested me, I shall come forth as gold" (23:10).

8. "He stretcheth out the north over the empty place, and hangeth the earth upon nothing" (26:7).

9. "Oh, that I knew where I might find him, that I might come even to his seat" (23:3)! This problem was solved through the incarnation of Christ! See John 1:18. Also see John 1:45.

10. "How then can man be justified with God? Or how can he be clean that is born of a woman?" Problem solved through the death of Christ! See Romans 4:24,25; 5:1.

11. "If a man die, shall he live again?" (Job 14:14)? Problem solved through the resurrection of Christ!

12. "For I know that my redeemer liveth, and that he shall stand at the latter day upon the earth: And though after my skin worms destroy this body, yet in my flesh shall I see God" (19:25,26).

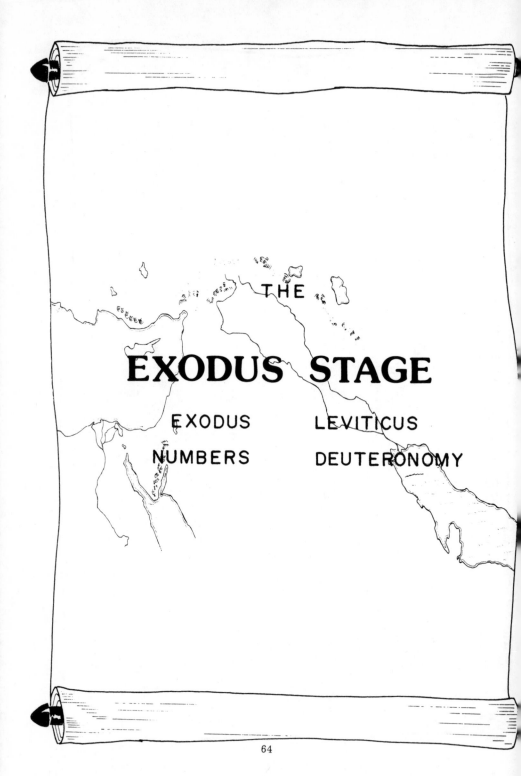

THE

# EXODUS STAGE

### EXODUS    LEVITICUS

### NUMBERS    DEUTERONOMY

# Exodus Stage

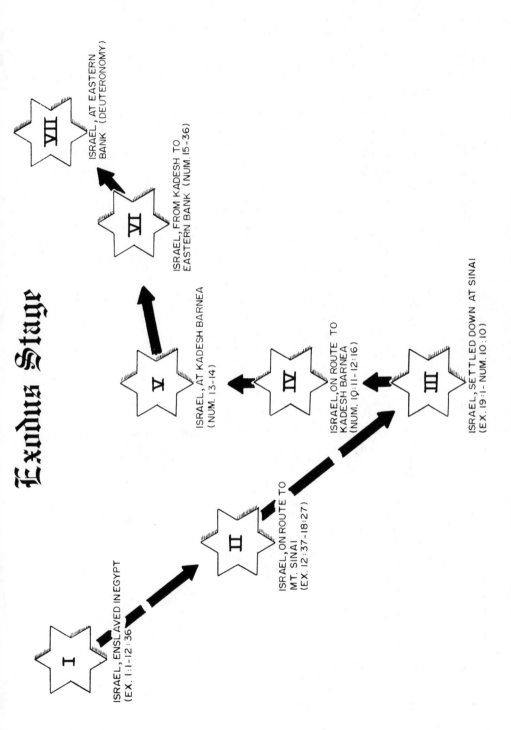

I — ISRAEL, ENSLAVED IN EGYPT (EX. 1:1-12:36)

II — ISRAEL, ON ROUTE TO MT. SINAI (EX. 12:37-18:27)

III — ISRAEL, SETTLED DOWN AT SINAI (EX. 19:1 - NUM. 10:10)

IV — ISRAEL, ON ROUTE TO KADESH BARNEA (NUM. 10:11-12:16)

V — ISRAEL, AT KADESH BARNEA (NUM. 13-14)

VI — ISRAEL, FROM KADESH TO EASTERN BANK (NUM. 15-36)

VII — ISRAEL, AT EASTERN BANK (DEUTERONOMY)

# Israel, Enslaved in Egypt

★ *GOD'S PEOPLE:* PERSECUTED BY A PHARAOH WHO KNEW NOT JOSEPH. (EX.I)

★ *GOD'S GRACE:* HE REMEMBERED HIS COVENANT WITH ABRAHAM AND HEARD THEIR CRIES. (2:23-25)

★ *GOD'S MAN:* *MOSES*

> *HIS FIRST 40 YEARS AS A PRINCE IN EGYPT* *(2:1-14)*
>
> HE IS RESCUED BY AN EGYPTIAN PRINCESS AS A BABY
>
> HE RESCUES AN ISRAELI SLAVE AS A MAN
>
> *HIS SECOND 40 YEARS AS A SHEPHERD IN MIDIAN (2:15-4:31)*
> HE MARRIES A GIRL NAMED ZIPPORAH
>
> HE RECEIVES HIS BURNING BUSH CALL

★ *GOD'S ENEMY:* PHARAOH REFUSES TO FREE THE JEWS AND INCREASES THEIR WORK BURDEN. (5:2,4-9)

★ *GOD'S PLAGUES:* EXODUS 7-10

| | Nature | Purpose | Egyptian god defeated | |
|---|---|---|---|---|
| I. | Water into blood | | OSIRIS | 7:20 |
| 2. | A Frog Invasion | I. TO SHOW ISRAEL THEIR TRUE GOD. | HEKT | 8:6 |
| 3. | Lice | | SEB | 8:17 |
| 4. | Flies | | HATKOK | 8:24 |
| 5. | Cattle disease | 2. TO SHOW EGYPT THEIR FALSE gods. | APIS | 9:6 |
| 6. | Boils | | TYPHON | 9:10 |
| 7. | Hail with Fire | | SHU | 9:24 |
| 8. | Locusts | | SERAPIA | 10:13 |
| 9. | 3-day darkness | | RA | 10:22 |
| 10. | Death of First Born | | ALL gods | 12:29 |

★ *GOD'S CHOICE*

| FACT | REASON |
|---|---|
| THAT THE FIRST BORN BE SANCTIFIED | HE WANTED A NATION OF PRIESTS |
| THAT THE SOUTHERN ROUTE BE TAKEN | ISRAEL NEEDED TO SPEND TIME WITH HIM. |

# ISRAEL, ON ROUTE TO MT. SINAI
## EX. 12-18

| | EVENT | DETAIL |
|---|---|---|
| A. | APPEARANCE OF GLORY CLOUD 13:21,22 | THE FIRST OF TEN BIBLICAL APPEARANCES |
| B. | CHASE BY PHARAOH 14:5-10 | THE DECISION OF THE PHARAOH- TO FOLLOW UP! |
| | | THE DESPAIR OF THE PEOPLE- TO GIVE UP! |
| | | THE DECLARATION OF THE PROPHET-TO LOOK UP! |
| C. | THE MIRACLE AT THE RED SEA 14:13-15:21 | THE CLOUDY PILLAR - *PROTECTING !* |
| | | THE RED SEA - *PARTING !* |
| | | THE EGYPTIAN ARMY - *PERISHING !* |
| | | THE LORD'S PEOPLE *PRAISING !* |
| D. | THE EPISODE AT MARAH 15:22-26 | THE GALLING WATERS |
| | | THE GOODLY TREE |
| | | **THE GREAT PHYSICIAN** |
| E. | THE GIVING OF MANNA 16:4,14,35 | THE SARCASTIC CROWD |
| | | THE SUPERNATURAL FOOD |
| F. | THE INSTITUTION OF THE SABBATH 16:23,26-30 | GIVEN TO ISRAEL AS A SPIRITUAL WEDDING RING |
| | | COMMEMORATED A FINISHED CREATION |
| G. | THE WATER FILLED ROCK 17:1-7 | IN OBEDIENCE MOSES STRIKES THIS ROCK |
| | | IN DISOBEDIENCE HE WILL LATER STRIKE ANOTHER ROCK SEE NUM. 20:7-13 |
| H. | VICTORY OVER THE AMALEKITES (4 "FIRSTS" NOW OCCUR) 17:8-16 | FIRST MENTION OF JOSHUA |
| | | FIRST INTERCESSION OF MOSES FOR ISRAEL |
| | | FIRST PART OF BIBLE TO BE WRITTEN (?) |
| | | FIRST REFERENCE TO GOD AS JEHOVAH-NISSI |
| I. | MOSES REUNITED WITH HIS FAMILY 18:5 | HE GREETS HIS FATHER-IN-LAW, WIFE AND 2 SONS. |

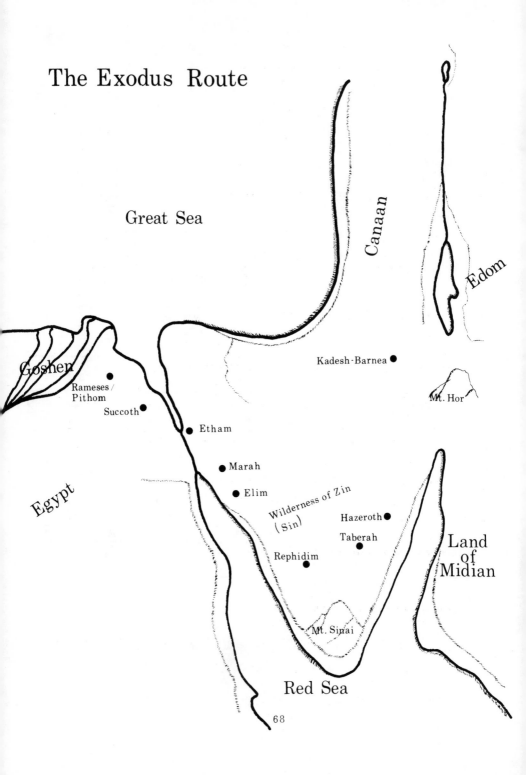

The Exodus Route

Great Sea

Canaan

Edom

Goshen

Rameses /
Pithom

Succoth

Etham

Marah

Elim

Egypt

Kadesh-Barnea

Mt. Hor

Wilderness of Zin
(Sin)

Hazeroth

Taberah

Rephidim

Land
of
Midian

Mt. Sinai

Red Sea

# ISRAEL, SETTLED DOWN AT SINAI

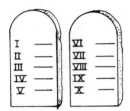

*ONE*

EX. 20:3-17

THE COMMANDMENTS OF THE LAW — REQUIREMENT FOR DIVINE FELLOWSHIP

*TWO*

EX. 32

THE CORRUPTION OF THE CALF – RUINATION OF DIVINE FELLOWSHIP

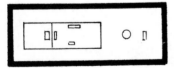

*THREE*   EX. 25-31,35-40

CONSTRUCTION OF THE TABERNACLE - RESTORATION TO DIVINE FELLOWSHIP

*THREE MAIN EVENTS OCCURRING AT SINAI*

# THE THREE-FOLD DIVISION OF THE LAW

| | MORAL CODE | SPIRITUAL CODE | SOCIAL CODE |
|---|---|---|---|
| I | THOU SHALT HAVE NO OTHER GODS BEFORE ME. | THIS SECTION DEALT WITH THOSE SPECIAL ORDINANCES WHICH FORE-SHADOWED CHRIST AND HIS FULL REDEMPTION. IT INCLUDED: | THIS SECTION INCLUDED RULES GOVERN-ING ISRAEL'S DIET, SANITATION, QUARANTINE, SOIL CONSERVATION, TAXATION, MILITARY SERVICE, MARRI-AGE, CHILDBIRTH, DIVORCE, ETC. |
| II | THOU SHALT NOT MAKE UNTO THEE ANY GRAVEN IMAGE. | | |
| III | THOU SHALT NOT TAKE THE NAME OF THE LORD THY GOD IN VAIN. | 1. THE SEVEN LEVITICAL FEASTS. | |
| IV | REMEMBER THE SABBATH DAY TO KEEP IT HOLY. | 2. THE FIVE LEVITICAL OFFERINGS | |
| V | HONOR THY FATHER AND THY MOTHER. | *Ex. 35-40, Leviticus* | *Book of Leviticus* |
| VI | THOU SHALT NOT KILL. | | |
| VII | THOU SHALT NOT COMMIT ADULTERY. | | |
| VIII | THOU SHALT NOT STEAL. | | |
| IX | THOU SHALT NOT BEAR FALSE WITNESS. | | |
| X | THOU SHALT NOT COVET. | | |
| | THE REVELATION FROM CHRIST<br><br>(I COR. 10:4) | THE REALIZATION IN CHRIST<br>(MAT. 5:17,18; ROM. 10:4; I COR. 5:7) | THE REGULATION UNTIL CHRIST<br><br>(GAL. 3:24) |

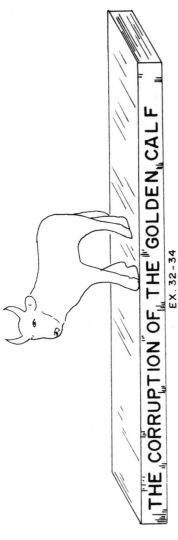

# THE CORRUPTION OF THE GOLDEN CALF

EX. 32-34

- MOSES ASCENDS MT. SINAI TO MEET WITH GOD.
- AARON IS PERSUADED TO MAKE A GOLDEN IDOL.
- ISRAEL INDULGES IN BOTH IDOLATRY AND IMMORALITY.
- GOD ANNOUNCES TO MOSES HIS INTENTION TO DESTROY ISRAEL.
- MOSES INTERCEDES FOR ISRAEL AND ENTERS THE CAMP BELOW.
- THE STONES OF THE LAW ARE BROKEN AND THE GOLDEN CALF IS BURNED.
- AARON IS REBUKED AND ISRAEL IS PUNISHED.
- THE LOYAL TRIBE OF LEVI IS CHOSEN FOR THE PRIESTHOOD.
- 3,000 CHIEF TROUBLEMAKERS ARE EXECUTED.
- MOSES ASCENDS SINAI AND VIEWS GOD'S GLORY FROM A CLEFT IN THE ROCK.
- HE DESCENDS SINAI CARRYING A NEW COPY OF THE LAW AND WEARING A SHINING FACE.

71

# THE CONSTRUCTION OF THE TABERNACLE

| | |
|---|---|
| DESCRIPTION AND SIZE | CONSISTED OF THREE SECTIONS: (1) OUTER COURT (2) INNER COURT (3) HOLY OF HOLIES |
| | OUTER COURT: SIMILAR TO A PICKET FENCE - 150 FT. LONG, 75 FT. WIDE, 7 1/2 FT. HIGH |
| | TENT WITHIN THE OUTER COURT - 45 FT. LONG, 15 FT. WIDE, 15 FT. HIGH |
| | TENT HAD TWO ROOMS WHICH WERE SEPARATED BY A THICK VEIL |
| | EASTERN TENT ROOM KNOWN AS THE INNER COURT OR HOLY PLACE |
| | WESTERN TENT ROOM KNOWN AS THE HOLY OF HOLIES |
| BUILDING MATERIALS | GOLD, SILVER, BRONZE, ANIMAL CLOTH, ACACIA WOOD, ONYX STONES |
| FURNITURE<br>EX. 25, 27, 30, 37, 38 | IN OUTER COURT: A BRONZE ALTAR AND A BRONZE LAVER |
| | IN INNER COURT: SHEWBREAD TABLE, LAMPSTAND, AND INCENSE ALTAR |
| | IN HOLY OF HOLIES: THE ARK OF THE COVENANT |
| TIME OF CONSTRUCTION | SIX MONTHS |
| METHOD OF CONSTRUCTION | MADE BY WILLING HANDS AND HEARTS - SEE EX. 35; NUM. 7 |
| THE PRIESTS<br>EX. 28-29 | HAD TO COME FROM THE TRIBE OF LEVI |
| | WERE ANOINTED WITH WATER, OIL, AND BLOOD |
| THE HIGH PRIEST | HAD TO COME FROM THE LINE OF AARON OF THE TRIBE OF LEVI |
| | CLOTHING: TWO EPHODS (OUTER AND INNER ROBES) BREASTPLATE, MITRE, URIM AND THUMMIN |
| | DUTIES: TO CARE FOR THE PHYSICAL NEEDS OF THE TABERNACLE AND THE SPIRITUAL NEEDS OF THE PEOPLE |

| OFFERINGS | | |
|---|---|---|
| BURNT OFFERING | LEV. 1 | |
| MEAL OFFERING | LEV. 2 | |
| PEACE OFFERING | LEV. 3 | OFFERED PRIMARILY TO MAINTAIN FELLOWSHIP WITH GOD. |
| SIN OFFERING | LEV. 4 | |
| TRESPASS OFFERING | LEV. 5 | OFFERED PRIMARILY TO RESTORE FELLOWSHIP TO GOD. |

| HOLY FEASTS (LEV. 23,25) | | |
|---|---|---|
| WEEKLY SABBATH | | |
| 7-YEAR SABBATH | | |
| 50-YEAR SABBATH | | THESE THREE SPEAK OF GOD'S FIRST GREAT WORK, THAT OF CREATION. SEE REV. 4:11 |
| PASSOVER | SPEAKS OF CALVARY | |
| FIRST FRUITS | THE RESURRECTION | |
| PENTECOST | COMING OF HOLY SPIRIT | |
| TRUMPETS | RAPTURE & 2ND. COMING | |
| ATONEMENT | THE TRIBULATION | |
| TABERNACLE | THE MILLENNIUM | THESE SIX SPEAK OF GOD'S SECOND GREAT WORK, THAT OF REDEMPTION. SEE REV. 5:9. |

**THE PURPOSE OF THE TABERNACLE**

To provide for ISRAEL a Visible Center of Worship.
To preview the Work of CHRIST. Note Similarities between the Language of MOSES and JOHN.

| MOSES | JOHN |
|---|---|
| DESCRIBES THE BRAZEN ALTAR | DESCRIBES THE LAMB OF GOD - JN. 1:29 |
| SPEAKS OF THE BRAZEN LAVER | SPEAKS OF THE WATER OF LIFE - JN. 4:14 |
| WRITES OF THE TABLE OF SHEWBREAD | WRITES OF THE BREAD OF LIFE - JN. 6:35 |
| TALKS OF THE LAMPSTAND | TALKS OF THE LIGHT OF THE WORLD - JN. 9:5 |
| PRESENTS THE ALTAR OF INCENSE | PRESENTS THE GREAT PRAYER OF CHRIST - JN. 17 |
| WITNESSES OF THE MERCY SEAT | WITNESS OF CHRIST OUR MERCY SEAT - 1 JN. 2:2 |

| | |
|---|---|
| **DEDICATION OF TABERNACLE** | *THE TRIUMPH:* GOD'S GLORY CLOUD FILLS THE PLACE – EXOD. 40:33-38<br>*THE TRAGEDY:* GOD'S JUDGMENT FALLS UPON AARON'S TWO WICKED SONS. – LEV. 10:1-11 |
| **CENSUS OF TABERNACLE** | THE FIRST OF TWO EXODUS CENSUS NOW TAKES PLACE (NUM. 1) FOR 2nd CENSUS SEE NUM. 26. |
| **NAZIRITE VOW** | 3 RULES: (1) NOT TO DRINK WINE (2) NOT TO CUT HAIR (3) AVOID CONTACT WITH DEAD OBJECTS. NUM. 6 |

## TABERNACLE PLAN

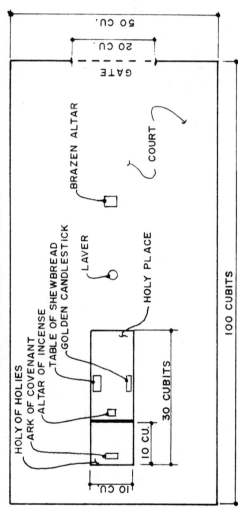

HOLY OF HOLIES
ARK OF COVENANT
ALTAR OF INCENSE
TABLE OF SHEWBREAD
GOLDEN CANDLESTICK
LAVER
BRAZEN ALTAR
HOLY PLACE
COURT
GATE
50 CU.
20 CU.
30 CUBITS
10 CU.
10 CU.
100 CUBITS

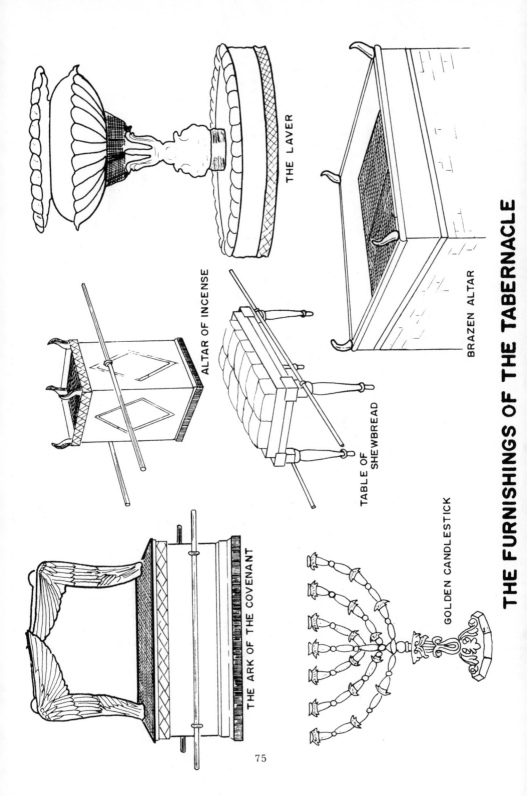

THE LAVER

ALTAR OF INCENSE

BRAZEN ALTAR

TABLE OF SHEWBREAD

THE ARK OF THE COVENANT

GOLDEN CANDLESTICK

**THE FURNISHINGS OF THE TABERNACLE**

75

# Tribal Encampment Position

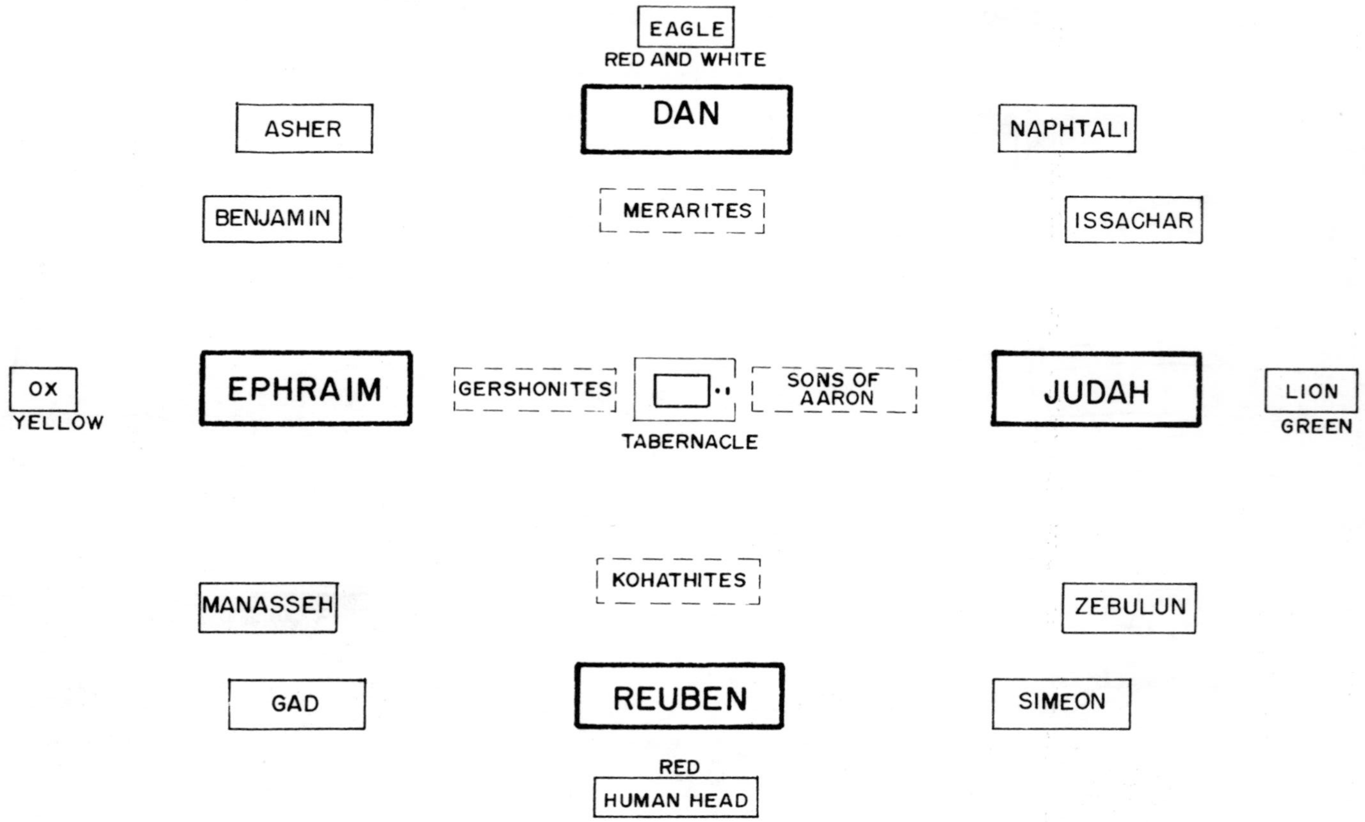

LION
GREEN

ISSACHAR

NAPHTALI

JUDAH

ZEBULUN

SIMEON

EAGLE
RED AND WHITE

DAN

MERARITES

SONS OF AARON

GERSHONITES

TABERNACLE

KOHATHITES

REUBEN

RED
HUMAN HEAD

ASHER

BENJAMIN

EPHRAIM

MANASSEH

GAD

OX
YELLOW

# ISRAEL ON ROUTE TO KADESH – BARNEA

*A SUFFERING SISTER*   (NUM. 12)

FOR CRITICIZING BOTH MOSES AND HIS WIFE
MIRIAM IS PUNISHED WITH LEPROSY.

*A DEADLY DIET*

TO SHOW THEIR HATRED FOR THE MANNA,
THE PEOPLE TURN TO A DIET OF QUAIL MEAT.
A DEADLY PLAGUE FOLLOWS. (NUM. II: 31-34)

*A PROVOKED PROPHET*

AT MOSES' REQUEST, GOD SENDS 70 MEN TO
HELP HIM. (NUM. II: 14-25)

*A MURMURING MIXT MULTITUDE*

GOD SENDS A FIERY PLAGUE TO STOP THE
BITTER AND BLASPHEMOUS COMPLAINTS
OF ISRAEL. (NUM. II: 1-3)

*A CONTINUING CLOUD*

GOD'S FAITHFUL GUIDE CONTINUED TO SHOW
THEM THE WAY.(NUM. 10:34-36)

*A BALKING BROTHER-IN-LAW.*   .

MOSES UNSUCCESSFULLY ATTEMPTS
TO SECURE THE SERVICES OF HIS
BROTHER-IN-LAW AS A GUIDE.
(NUM. 10:29-31)

MOUNT
SINAI

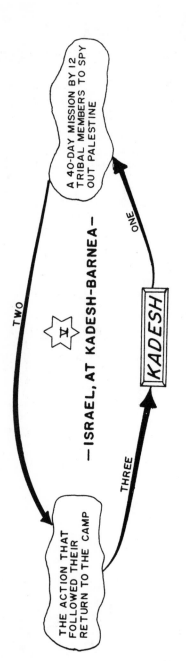

THE ACTION THAT FOLLOWED THEIR RETURN TO THE CAMP

A 40-DAY MISSION BY 12 TRIBAL MEMBERS TO SPY OUT PALESTINE

— ISRAEL, AT KADESH-BARNEA —

KADESH

ONE   TWO   THREE

| | | | NUMBERS |
|---|---|---|---|
| THE 2-FOLD REPORT | 10 MAN MAJORITY REPORT | "WE ARE NOT ABLE TO GO UP AGAINST...THE PEOPLE; FOR THEY ARE STRONGER THAN WE." | 13:31 |
| | | "AND THERE WE SAW GIANTS ...AND WE WERE... AS GRASSHOPPERS ....IN THEIR SIGHT." | 13:33 |
| | 2 MAN MINORITY REPORT | "LET US GO UP AT ONCE, AND POSSESS IT; FOR WE ARE WELL ABLE TO OVERCOME IT." | 13:30 |
| | | "...NEITHER FEAR YE THE PEOPLE OF THE LAND... FOR....THE LORD IS WITH US ..." | 14:9 |
| THE 2-FOLD REACTION | THE REACTION OF THE PEOPLE | "WOULD GOD THAT WE HAD DIED IN THE LAND OF EGYPT!" | 14:2 |
| | | "LET US MAKE A CAPTAIN, AND LET US RETURN INTO EGYPT." | 14:4 |
| | | THIS MARKED THEIR 10th REBELLION AGAINST HIM. | 14:22 |
| | THE REACTION OF GOD | THEIR CARCASSES WOULD FALL IN THE WILDERNESS. | 14:29 |
| | | NO ONE OVER 20 (JOSHUA & CALEB EXCEPTED) WOULD ENTER PALESTINE. | 14:29 |
| | | THEY WOULD WANDER 40 YEARS, A YEAR FOR EACH DAY THE SPIES SPENT IN THE LAND. | 14:34 |
| | | THE MAJORITY REPORT MEMBERS WOULD DIE OF A PLAGUE. | 14:37 |

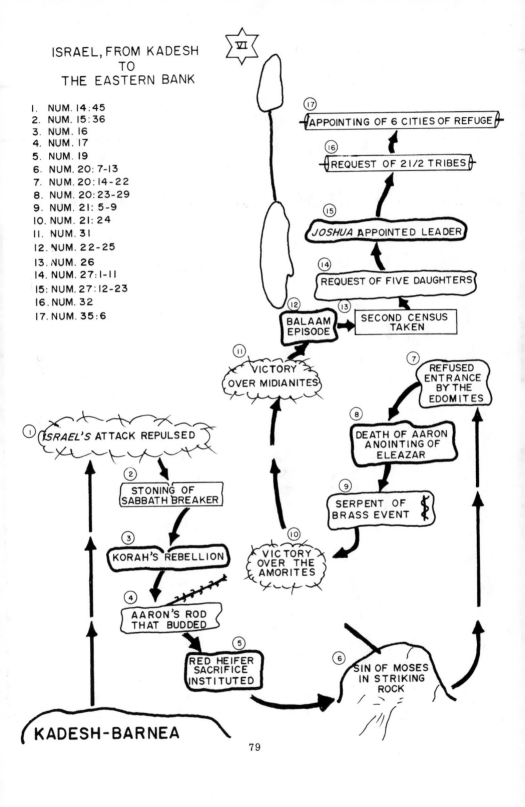

ISRAEL, FROM KADESH
TO
THE EASTERN BANK

VI

1. NUM. 14:45
2. NUM. 15:36
3. NUM. 16
4. NUM. 17
5. NUM. 19
6. NUM. 20:7-13
7. NUM. 20:14-22
8. NUM. 20:23-29
9. NUM. 21:5-9
10. NUM. 21:24
11. NUM. 31
12. NUM. 22-25
13. NUM. 26
14. NUM. 27:1-11
15. NUM. 27:12-23
16. NUM. 32
17. NUM. 35:6

17 APPOINTING OF 6 CITIES OF REFUGE

16 REQUEST OF 2 1/2 TRIBES

15 JOSHUA APPOINTED LEADER

14 REQUEST OF FIVE DAUGHTERS

12 BALAAM EPISODE

13 SECOND CENSUS TAKEN

11 VICTORY OVER MIDIANITES

7 REFUSED ENTRANCE BY THE EDOMITES

1 ISRAEL'S ATTACK REPULSED

2 STONING OF SABBATH BREAKER

8 DEATH OF AARON ANOINTING OF ELEAZAR

3 KORAH'S REBELLION

9 SERPENT OF BRASS EVENT

4 AARON'S ROD THAT BUDDED

10 VICTORY OVER THE AMORITES

5 RED HEIFER SACRIFICE INSTITUTED

6 SIN OF MOSES IN STRIKING ROCK

KADESH-BARNEA

# ISRAEL
# AT THE EASTERN BANK
# Book of Deuteronomy

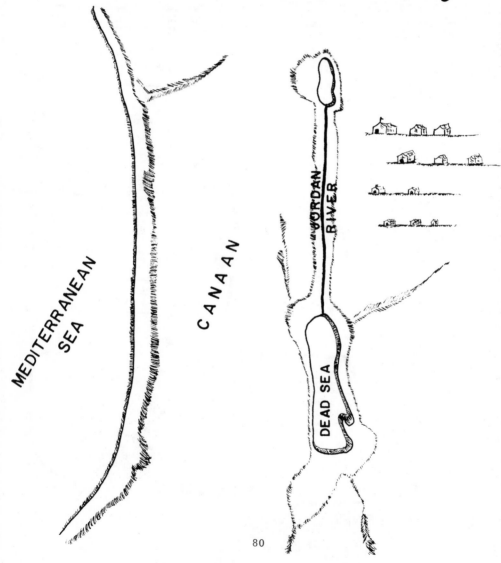

# The BOOK of DEUTERONOMY—MOSES' FINAL ACCOMPLISHMENTS

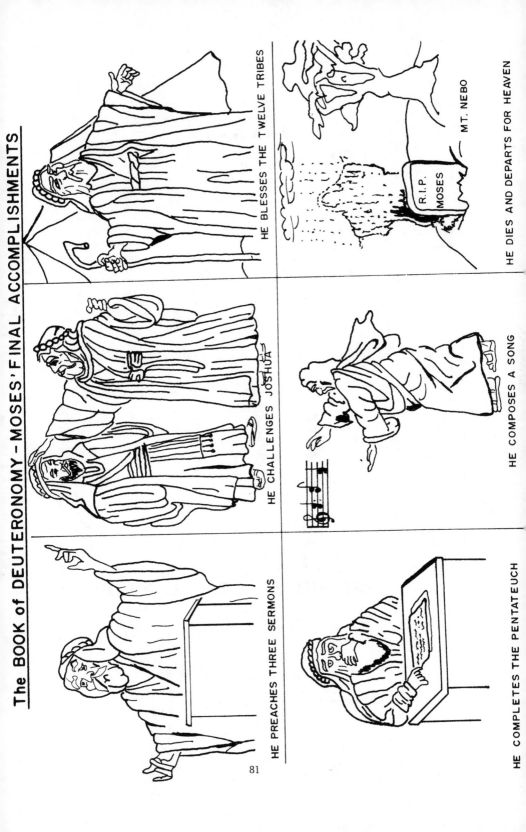

HE PREACHES THREE SERMONS

HE CHALLENGES JOSHUA

HE BLESSES THE TWELVE TRIBES

HE COMPLETES THE PENTATEUCH

HE COMPOSES A SONG

R.I.P. MOSES

MT. NEBO

HE DIES AND DEPARTS FOR HEAVEN

81

## FIRST SERMON (1-4)

| POINT STRESSED | REFERENCE |
|---|---|
| THE SPLENDOR OF GOD THEY HAD EXPERIENCED AT MT. SINAI. | 4:10-19, 32,33 |
| A REVIEW OF THEIR TRAGIC SIN AT KADESH-BARNEA | 1:2, 27 |
| A REVIEW OF HIS OWN SIN WHICH WOULD KEEP HIM FROM CANAAN | 3:23-27; 4:21,2? |
| A CHALLENGE FOR ISRAEL TO ENCOURAGE JOSHUA | 1:38; 3:28 |
| A SETTING APART OF THE THREE EASTERN CITIES OF REFUGE | 4:41-43 |

## SECOND SERMON (5-26)

| POINT STRESSED | REFERENCE |
|---|---|
| REPEATING OF THE TEN COMMANDMENTS | 5:7-21 |
| WARNING AGAINST (1) IMMORALITY (2) COMPROMISE (3) WITCHCRAFT | 23:17; 7:1-5; 18:9-14 |
| GIVING A DESCRIPTION OF CANAAN | 8:7-8 |
| REVIEWING HIS PERSONAL EXPERIENCE WITH GOD ON SINAI | 9:9-21 |
| REMINDING ISRAEL OF THEIR FINANCIAL OBLIGATIONS TO GOD | CHAPTER 26 |
| GIVING LAWS CONCERNING (1) CLOTHING (2) DIVORCE (3) WOMAN'S RIGHTS (4) WARFARE | 22:5; 24:1-4; 21:10-17; 22:13-20; 20:1-20 |
| SUMMARIZING GOD'S OVER-ALL PURPOSE FOR THEIR GENERATION | 6:23 |

## THIRD SERMON (27-30)

| POINT STRESSED | REFERENCE |
|---|---|
| A COMMAND TO THE LEVITES UPON CROSSING INTO JORDAN | 11:26-29; 27:1-1? |
| *THE BLESSINGS OF THE LAW TO BE READ ON MT. GERIZIM | 28:1-14 |
| *THE CURSES OF THE LAW TO BE READ ON MT. EBAL | 27:15-26; 28:15-6 |
| A DISCUSSION OF THE 7-FOLD FEATURES OF THE PALESTINIAN COVENANT. | CHAPTERS 28-3? |
| *ISRAEL TO BE DISPERSED FOR DISOBEDIENCE | 28:36, 49-53, 63-68; 30:1 |
| *ISRAEL TO REPENT WHILE IN DISPERSION | 30:2 |
| *THE RETURN OF CHRIST TO OCCUR | 30:3 |
| *ISRAEL TO BE RESTORED TO THE LAND | 30:5 |
| *THE NATION TO RECEIVE A NEW HEART | 30:6 |
| *ISRAEL'S OPPRESSORS WILL BE JUDGED | 30:7. |
| *ISRAEL TO EXPERIENCE PROSPERITY | 30:9 |

# HE PREACHES THREE SERMONS

# MOSES THE THEOLOGIAN

During these THREE SERMONS MOSES Expounds upon TEN GREAT Theological Themes.

1. THE *FAITHFULNESS* OF GOD (2:7; 4:33-38; 7:6-8; 8:3-4; 9:4-6; 29:5-6; 32:9-14)

2. THE *WORD* OF GOD (4:1,2,7,9; 11:18-21; 30:11-14)

3. THE *PERSON* OF GOD (6:4,5; 7:9; 32:39)

4. THE *LOVE* OF GOD (7:13)

5. THE *GLORY* OF GOD (4:39; 10:17,18)

6. THE *GRACE* OF GOD (7:6-9; 9:4-6)

7. THE COMING *GREAT PROPHET* OF GOD (18:15-19)

8. THE *WILL* OF GOD (10:12-16)

9. THE *KINGS* OF GOD (17:14-20)

10. THE *ISRAEL* OF GOD (4:25-31; 11:16,17)

# HE CHALLENGES JOSHUA

DEUTERONOMY 31

7  And Moses called unto Joshua, and said unto him in the sight of all Israel, Be strong and of a good courage: for thou must go with this people unto the land which the LORD hath sworn unto their fathers to give them; and thou shalt cause them to inherit it.
8  And the LORD, he it is that doth go before thee; he will be with thee, he will not fail thee, neither forsake thee: fear not, neither be dismayed.

14  And the LORD said unto Moses, Behold, thy days approach that thou must die: call Joshua, and present yourselves in the tabernacle of the congregation, that I may give him a charge. And Moses and Joshua went, and presented themselves in the tabernacle of the congregation.

# HE COMPLETES THE PENTATEUCH

## DEUTERONOMY 31

9    And Moses wrote this law, and delivered it unto the priests the sons of Levi, which bare the ark of the covenant of the LORD, and unto all the elders of Israel.

24    And it came to pass when Moses had made an end of writing the words of this law in a book, until they were finished.

# HE BLESSES THE TWELVE TRIBES

DEUTERONOMY 33

1. AND this *is* the blessing, where-with Moses the man of God blessed the children of Israel before his death.

2. And he said, The LORD came from Sinai, and rose up from Seir unto them; he shined forth from mount Paran, and he came with ten thousands of saints: from his right hand *went* a fiery law for them.

3. Yea, he loved the people; all his saints *are* in thy hand: and they sat down at thy feet; *every one* shall receive of thy words.

27. The eternal God *is thy* refuge, and underneath *are* the everlasting arms; and he shall thrust out the enemy from before thee; and shall say, Destroy *them*.

28. Israel then shall dwell in safety alone: the fountain of Jacob *shall be* upon a land of corn and wine; also his heavens shall drop down dew.

29. Happy *art* thou, O Israel: who *is* like unto thee, O people saved by the LORD, the shield of thy help, and who *is* the sword of thy excellency! and thine enemies shall be found liars unto thee; and thou shalt tread upon their high places.

# —HE COMPOSES A SONG—

DEUTERONOMY

## *THE PURPOSE FOR THE SONG*

19    Now therefore write ye this song for you, and teach it the children of Israel: put it in their mouths, that this song may be a witness for me against the children of Israel. (31:19)

## *THE MAIN THEME OF THE SONG*

3    Because I will publish the name of the LORD: ascribe ye greatness unto our God.

4    He *is* the Rock, his work *is* perfect: for all his ways *are* judgment: a God of truth and without iniquity, just and right *is* he.

9    For the LORD'S portion *is* his people; Jacob *is* the lot of his inheritance.

10   He found him in a desert land, and in the waste howling wilderness; he led him about, he instructed him, he kept him as the apple of his eye.

11   As an eagle stirreth up her nest, fluttereth over her young, spreadeth abroad her wings, taketh them, beareth them on her wings:

43   Rejoice, O ye nations, with his people: for he will avenge the blood of his servants, and will render vengeance to his adversaries, and will be merciful unto his land, *and* to his people. (32:3,4,9,10,11,43)

# HE DIES AND DEPARTS FOR HEAVEN

MT. NEBO

DEUTERONOMY 34

1 AND Moses went up from the plains of Moab unto the mountain of Nebo, to the top of Pisgah, that is over against Jericho. And the LORD shewed him all the land of Gil-e-ad, unto Dan.

5 So Moses the Servant of the LORD died there in the land of Moab, according to the word of the LORD.

6 And he buried him in a valley in the land of Moab, over against Beth-peor: but no man knoweth of his sepulchre unto this day.

7 And Moses was an hundred and twenty years old when he died: his eye was not dim, nor his natural force abated.

10 And there arose not a prophet since in Israel like unto Moses, whom the LORD knew face to face,

# THE
# CONQUEST STAGE

## JOSHUA

# THE BOOK OF JOSHUA

**Invasion of The Land**

ISRAEL CLAIMS ITS POSSESSIONS
JOSHUA 1-5

**Subjection of The Land**

ISRAEL CONQUERS ITS POSSESSIONS
JOSHUA 6-12

**Distribution of The Land**

ISRAEL COLONIZES ITS POSSESSIONS
JOSHUA 13-24

## INVASION OF THE LAND

| EVENT | EXPLANATION |
|---|---|
| THE PREPARATION 1:1-9 | GOD SPEAKS TO JOSHUA: *MOSES WAS DEAD, BUT GOD WOULD BE WITH HIM.* JOSHUA SPEAKS TO ISRAEL: *GET PREPARED, FOR WE MOVE OUT IN 3 DAYS.* |
| THE PENETRATION 2:1-24 | TWO ISRAELI SPIES SEARCH OUT JERICHO. UPON BEING DISCOVERED THEY ARE HIDDEN BY A NEWLY-CONVERTED HARLOT NAMED RAHAB. |
| THE PASSAGE 3:1-17 | THE MESSAGE FROM GOD: *STEP OUT AS IF THE JORDAN WAS SOLID ROCK.* THE MIRACLE FROM GOD: *THE WATERS OF THE JORDAN ARE ROLLED BACK.* |
| THE PILE OF STONES 4:1-24 | ISRAEL WAS TO PLACE 12 HUGE STONES ON THE WESTERN BANK AS A MEMORIAL REMINDER OF THE SUPERNATURAL CROSSING. |
| THE PURIFICATION 5:2-9 | UPON REACHING THE WESTERN BANK THE ISRAELI MALES ARE CIRCUMCISED |
| THE PASSOVER 5:10 | THE PASSOVER IS OBSERVED UPON THE PLAINS OF JERICHO |
| THE PASSING DIET 5:11-12 | THE MANNA CEASES AND THEY EAT THE FOOD OF THE PROMISED LAND. |
| THE PRINCE FROM HEAVEN 5:13-15 | *JOSHUA IS VISITED AND REASSURED BY JESUS HIMSELF.* |

# SUBJECTION OF THE LAND

**NORTHERN**

**JOSHUA 11**

1. HAZOR, A CAPITOL BURNED DOWN
2. MEROM, SOME HORSES SLOWED DOWN

PHASE THREE

**CENTRAL**

**JOSHUA 6-8**

1. JERICHO, A CITY SHOUTED DOWN
2. AI, ARROGANCE KNOCKED DOWN
3. ACHOR, A SINNER SOUGHT DOWN
4. GERIZIM & EBAL, THE LAW HANDED DOWN

PHASE ONE

**SOUTHERN**

**JOSHUA 9-10**

1. GIBEON, THE WOOL PULLED DOWN
2. AJALON, THE SUN SHONE DOWN
3. MAKKEDAH, FIVE KINGS CUT DOWN

PHASE TWO

JORDAN RIVER

# DISTRIBUTION OF THE LAND

● *THE LAND DIVIDED (14:1-2; 19:51)*

| WEST OF JORDAN | EAST OF JORDAN | LAND FOR LEVI |
|---|---|---|
| ONE HALF TRIBE OF MANASSEH | | No Land given, for GOD Himself would be its Portion (13:33). However, LEVI was to receive 48 Special Cities from the 11 Tribes. (21:41) |
| EPHRAIM | | |
| JUDAH | *REUBEN* | |
| BENJAMIN | | |
| SIMEON | | |
| ZEBULUN | | |
| ISSACHAR | *GAD* | |
| ASHER | | |
| NAPHTALI | *ONE HALF TRIBE OF MANASSEH* | |
| DAN | | |
| *LAND WAS DIVIDED BY JOSHUA AND HIGH PRIEST THROUGH THE CASTING OF LOTS* | | |

● A WARRIOR EXCITED (14:7-12)

CALEB VISITS JOSHUA AND RELATES ONE OF SCRIPTURE'S MOST THRILLING TESTIMONIES.

● AN ALTAR INDICTED (CHAP. 22)
1. THE TABERNACLE WAS SET UP IN PALESTINE AT SHILOH (18:1)
2. THE 2 1/2 EASTERN TRIBES SET UP AN ALTAR ON JORDAN BANK AS A REMINDER OF THEIR COMMON HERITAGE WITH THE WESTERN TRIBES.
3. THIS WAS AT FIRST MISINTERPRETED AS AN ACT OF REBELLION AND A CIVIL WAR WAS NARROWLY AVERTED.

● A FINAL SERMON RECITED (23-24)
JOSHUA'S LAST WORDS TO ISRAEL.

# The Land of The Twelve Tribes

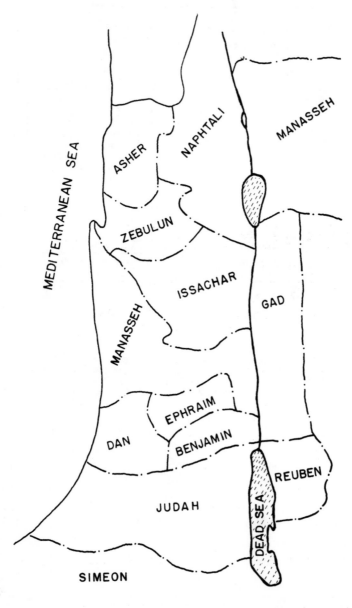

MEDITERRANEAN SEA

ASHER

NAPHTALI

MANASSEH

ZEBULUN

ISSACHAR

GAD

MANASSEH

EPHRAIM

DAN

BENJAMIN

REUBEN

JUDAH

DEAD SEA

SIMEON

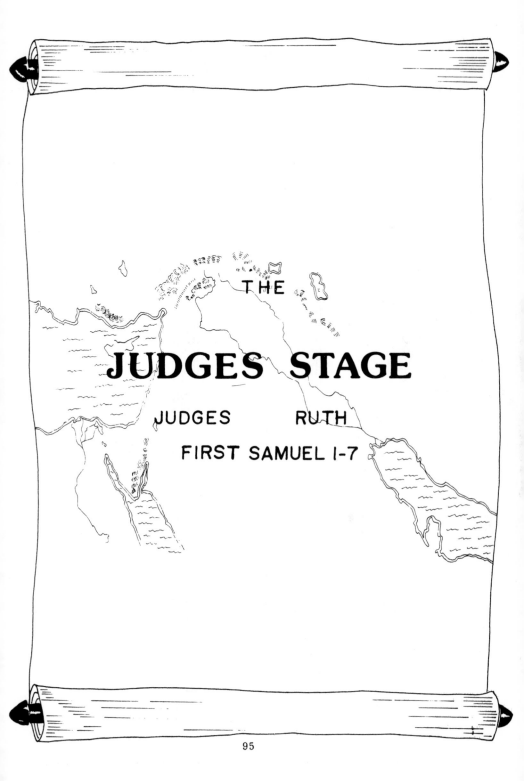

THE

# JUDGES STAGE

JUDGES          RUTH

FIRST SAMUEL 1-7

# JUDGES

THE ACTION DURING THIS PERIOD CENTERS AROUND NINE INDIVIDUALS OR GROUP OF INDIVIDUALS.

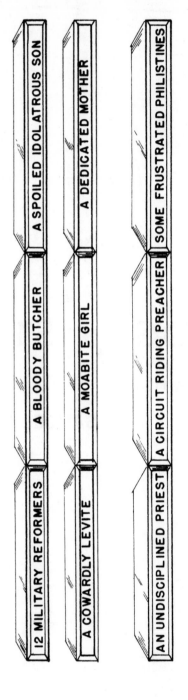

12 MILITARY REFORMERS — A BLOODY BUTCHER — A SPOILED IDOLATROUS SON

A COWARDLY LEVITE — A MOABITE GIRL — A DEDICATED MOTHER

AN UNDISCIPLINED PRIEST — A CIRCUIT RIDING PREACHER — SOME FRUSTRATED PHILISTINES

# 12 MILITARY REFORMERS

| NAME | OPPRESSING NATION | DURATION | REST | ACCOMPLISHMENTS |
|---|---|---|---|---|
| OTHNIEL (1:12,13; 3:8-10) | MESOPOTAMIA | 8 YRS. | 40 YRS. | WAS BOTH NEPHEW AND SON-IN-LAW OF CALEB. CAPTURED A STRONG CANAANITE CITY. |
| EHUD (3:12-30) | MOAB | 18 YRS. | 80 YRS. | ASSASSINATED A FAT MOABITE ENEMY KING NAMED EGLON. ORGANIZED AN ISRAELI ARMY WHICH KILLED 10,000 ENEMY TROOPS. |
| SHAMGAR (3:31) | PHILISTIA | UNRECORDED | UNRECORDED | KILLE 600 PHILISTINES WITH AN OXGOAD |
| BARAK (4-5) | CANAANITES | 20 YRS. | 40 YRS. | RAISED AN ARMY OF 10,000 AT DEBORAH'S ENCOURAGEMENT. DEFEATED ENEMY GENERAL NAMED SISERA AT BASE OF MT. TABOR. SISERA IS KILLED LATER BY JAEL WHILE IN HER TENT SLEEPING. BARAK AND DEBORAH SING A DUET OF PRAISE OVER THEIR VICTORY. |
| GIDEON (6-8) | MIDIAN | 7 YRS. | 40 YRS. | COMMISSIONED BY GOD TO DEFEAT THE MIDIANITES. PREPARE FOR THIS BY DESTROYING THE FAMILY IDOLS. THROWS OUT THE FLEECE TWICE. RAISES AN ARMY OF 10,000 SEES THIS ARMY REDUCED TO 300 BY GOD DEFEATS 135,000 ENEMY TROOPS WITH HIS 300. CAUSES ISRAEL TO SIN BY MAKING A GOLDEN EPHOD. |
| TOLA (10:1) | UNRECORDED | UNRECORDED | 23 YRS. | UNRECORDED |
| JAIR (10:3-5) | UNRECORDED | UNRECORDED | 22 YRS. | HE AND HIS 30 SONS DELIVERED 30 ISRAEL CITIES FROM OPPRESSION. |
| JEPHTHAH (10:6-12:17) | AMMON | 18 YRS. | 6 YRS. | WAS A HARLOT'S SON WHO BECAME A MIGHTY WARRIOR. ON THE EVE OF BATTLE HE MADE A RASH VOW TO GOD. IF VICTORIOUS HE WOULD OFFER THE FIRST THING THAT GREETED HIM. HIS DAUGHTER MET HIM AND HE SADLY PERFORMED HIS VOW. HE IS LATER PROVOKED INTO BATTLE WITH THE JEALOUS TRIBE OF EPHRAIM. |

| NAME | OPPRESSING NATION | DURATION | REST | ACCOMPLISHMENTS |
|---|---|---|---|---|
| IBZAN (12:8-10) | UNRECORDED | UNRECORDED | 7 YRS. | UNRECORDED |
| ELON (12:11,12) | UNRECORDED | UNRECORDED | 10 YRS. | UNRECORDED |
| ABDON (12:13-15) | UNRECORDED | UNRECORDED | 8 YRS. | UNRECORDED |
| SAMSON (13-16) | PHILISTIA | 40 YRS. | 20 YRS. | HE WAS TO BE RAISED AS A NAZARITE. HE KILLED A LION ON ROUTE TO HIS WEDDING. HE KILLED 30 PHILISTINES TO PAY OFF A CLOTHING DEBT. UPON LOSING HIS WIFE HE BURNS THE WHEAT FIELDS OF THE PHILISTINES. HE KILLS 1000 PHILISTINES WITH THE JAWBONE OF AN ASS. HE RIPS OFF AN IRON GATE AT GAZA. HE IS BETRAYED INTO THE HANDS OF THE PHILISTINES BY DELILAH. HE IS SHAVEN, BLINDED AND ENSLAVED. HE IS SUPERNATURALLY EMPOWERED TO DESTROY MANY PHILISTINES IN THEIR OWN TEMPLE BY PULLING IT DOWN. HE IS HIMSELF KILLED AT THIS TIME. |

# A TERRIBLE TRIO

## ABIMELECH, THE BLOODY BUTCHER — JUDGES 9

1. HE WAS THE MAD-DOG SON OF GIDEON
2. HE ARRANGED FOR THE MURDER OF 69 OF HIS HALF-BROTHERS. ONLY A MAN NAMED JOTHAM ESCAPED.
3. HE SET UP HIS "KINGDOM" AT SHECHEM.
4. HE WAS LATER KILLED BY GOD WHO USED AN EVIL SPIRIT AND AN OLD WOMAN TO PERFORM HIS WILL.

## MICAH, A MOTHER-SPOILED THIEF AND IDOL WORSHIPPER JUDGES 17-18

1. HE IS ENCOURAGED BY HIS INDULGENT MOTHER TO "START HIS OWN RELIGION."
2. HE DOES THIS BY HIRING HIS OWN PERSONAL PRIEST, A MONEY-HUNGRY LEVITE FROM BETHLEHEM.
3. THIS PERVERTED "PRIVATE PASTOR" IS LATER ENTICED BY THE TRIBE OF DAN TO BECOME THEIR OFFICIAL PRIEST.

## A COWARDLY AND EMOTIONALLY SICK LEVITE — JUDGES 19-21

1. A LEVITE AND HIS CONCUBINE ARE THREATENED BY A MOB OF SEX PERVERTS WHILE VISITING IN THE LAND OF BENJAMIN.
2. HE SAVES HIS MISERABLE HIDE BY ALLOWING THIS CORRUPT CROWD TO SEXUALLY MURDER THE WOMAN.
3. HE THEN CUTS UP HER DEAD BODY INTO TWELVE PIECES AND SENDS A BLOODLY CHUNK TO EACH TRIBE IN ISRAEL.
4. AN ARMY OF 450,000 IS RAISED BUT THE BENJAMIN TRIBE OFFICIALS REFUSE TO HAND OVER THE GUILTY MEN.
5. A CIVIL WAR BREAKS OUT WHICH LEAVES BUT 600 BENJAMINITE SOLDIERS ALIVE.
6. A PLAN IS EFFECTED BY THE ELEVEN TRIBES TO PROVIDE WIVES FOR THESE 600, LEST THE TRIBE OF BENJAMIN DISAPPEAR.

**A Moabite Girl**

| CHAPTER | CONTENT |
|---|---|
| ONE<br>RUTH<br>RENOUNCING | • A CITIZEN FROM BETHLEHEM NAMED ELIMELECH, HIS WIFE NAOMI AND THEIR TWO SONS MOVE TO MOAB DURING A FAMINE.<br><br>• THE BOYS MARRY MOABITE GIRLS, BUT SOON BOTH FATHER AND SONS DIE, LEAVING THREE WIDOWS.<br><br>• NAOMI RETURNS TO BETHLEHEM, ACCOMPANIED BY ONE OF HER DAUGHTERS-IN-LAW NAMED RUTH WHO HAD RENOUNCED HER MOABITE gods FOR THE TRUE GOD OF ISRAEL. |
| TWO<br>RUTH<br>REAPING | • IN THE PROVIDENCE OF GOD RUTH GLEANS WHEAT IN A FIELD OWNED BY BOAZ, A NEAR RELATIVE OF ELIMELECH.<br>• AT THEIR FIRST MEETING BOAZ FALLS IN LOVE WITH RUTH.<br>• UPON LEARNING OF THIS, NAOMI BEGINS PLANNING FOR THE WEDDING. |
| THREE<br>RUTH<br>RESTING | • NAOMI SENDS RUTH TO BOAZ THAT SHE MIGHT REQUEST OF HIM TO FULFILL HIS RESPONSIBILITY AS A KINSMAN REDEEMER.<br>• BOAZ IS THRILLED WITH RUTH'S REQUEST, BUT TELLS HER THERE IS A KINSMAN REDEEMER CLOSER THAN HE.<br>• RUTH RETURNS HOME AND LEAVES THE MATTER WITH GOD. |
| FOUR<br>RUTH<br>REJOICING | • BOAZ ARRANGES A MEETING WITH THE CLOSER KINSMAN REDEEMER.<br>• UPON HEARING THE FACTS HE STEPS ASIDE AND ALLOWS BOAZ TO FULFILL THE KINSMAN REDEEMER RESPONSIBILI-TIES, INCLUDING MARRIAGE TO RUTH.<br>• RUTH PRESENTS BOAZ WITH A MALE BABY WHICH IS NAMED OBED. |

# HANNAH

## THE

## SORROWING SINGING

## SAINT

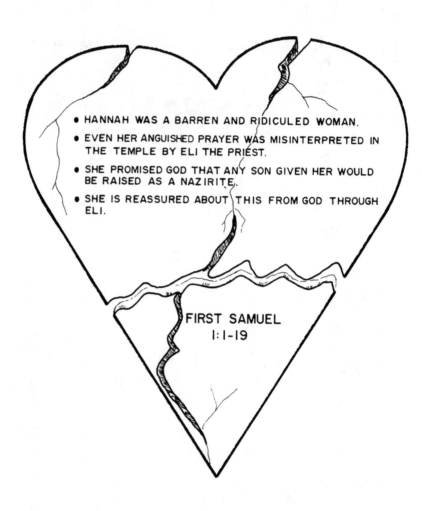

- HANNAH WAS A BARREN AND RIDICULED WOMAN.
- EVEN HER ANGUISHED PRAYER WAS MISINTERPRETED IN THE TEMPLE BY ELI THE PRIEST.
- SHE PROMISED GOD THAT ANY SON GIVEN HER WOULD BE RAISED AS A NAZIRITE.
- SHE IS REASSURED ABOUT THIS FROM GOD THROUGH ELI.

FIRST SAMUEL
1:1-19

## HER SORROW OF HEART

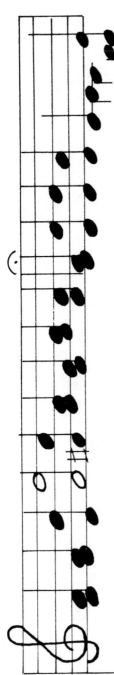

1. HANNAH GIVES BIRTH TO SAMUEL

2. UPON WEANING HIM SHE BRINGS HIM TO ELI FOR TEMPLE SERVICE UNTO GOD.

3. SHE SINGS A HYMN OF PRAISE TO GOD FOR:
   ● BLESSING THE POOR AND HUMBLE OVER THE RICH AND PROUD.
   ● KEEPING THE FEET OF HIS SAINTS.
   ● RIGHTFULLY JUDGING THE EARTH.

4. IN HER HYMN SHE UTTERS A MESSIANIC PROPHECY:
   "HE SHALL GIVE STRENGTH UNTO HIS KING, AND EXALT THE HORN OF HIS ANOINTED." (2:10)

5. HANNAH THEN BORE THREE ADDITIONAL SONS AND TWO DAUGHTERS.

(1st. SAM. I:20-2:II, 18-21)

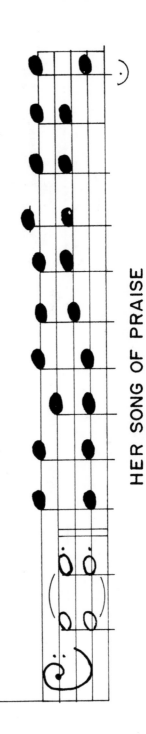

# HER SONG OF PRAISE
## I SAM. I, 2

# THE TRAVELING ARK

(SOME FRUSTRATED PHILISTINES)

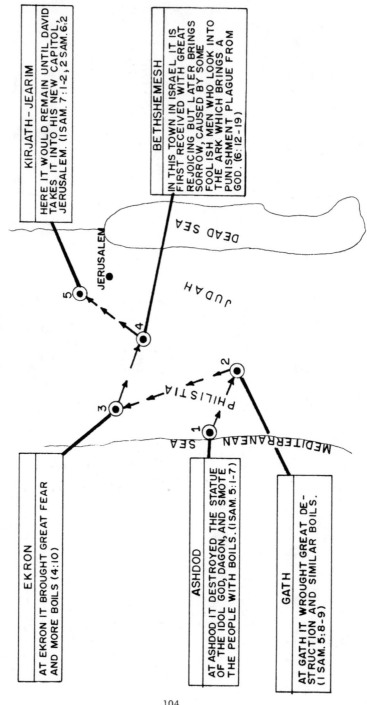

**KIRJATH-JEARIM**

HERE IT WOULD REMAIN UNTIL DAVID TAKES IT INTO HIS NEW CAPITOL, JERUSALEM. (I SAM. 7:1-2, 2 SAM. 6:2

**BETHSHEMESH**

IN THIS TOWN IN ISRAEL IT IS FIRST RECEIVED WITH GREAT REJOICING BUT LATER BRINGS SORROW, CAUSED BY SOME FOOLISH MEN WHO LOOK INTO THE ARK WHICH BRINGS A PUNISHMENT PLAGUE FROM GOD. (6:12-19)

DEAD SEA

JERUSALEM

JUDAH

PHILISTIA

MEDITERRANEAN SEA

**EKRON**

AT EKRON IT BROUGHT GREAT FEAR AND MORE BOILS (4:10)

**ASHDOD**

AT ASHDOD IT DESTROYED THE STATUE OF THE IDOL GOD, DAGON, AND SMOTE THE PEOPLE WITH BOILS. (I SAM. 5:1-7)

**GATH**

AT GATH IT WROUGHT GREAT DE-STRUCTION AND SIMILAR BOILS. (I SAM. 5:8-9)

104

# ELI

## THE UNDISCIPLINED PRIEST FATHER

| SINS OF HIS SONS | WARNINGS TO HIS SONS | DEATH OF HIS SONS |
|---|---|---|
| • THEY WERE UNSAVED (I SAM. 2:12) | • BY GOD THROUGH AN UNNAMED PROPHET (2:34) | • ISRAEL IS DEFEATED BY THE PHILISTINES (I SAM. 4:1-10) |
| • THEY REGARDED BELIAL AS THE TRUE GOD (2:12) | • BY GOD THROUGH THE LAD SAMUEL (3:1-18) | • THE ARK OF GOD IS CAPTURED (4:11) |
| • THEY STOLE THE OFFERINGS FROM GOD (2:14) | | • ELI'S SONS ARE KILLED (4:11) |
| • THEY BULLIED THE PEOPLE OF GOD (2:14) | | • ELI LEARNS OF THIS, FALLS FROM HIS SEAT AND DIES (4:12-18) |
| • THEY COMMITTED ADULTERY RIGHT IN THE TABERNACLE (2:22) | | • HIS DAUGHTER-IN-LAW DIES IN CHILDBIRTH, BUT NOT BEFORE NAMING HER BABY BOY ICHABOD (4:19-22) |
| • THEY CAUSED GOD'S PEOPLE TO TRANSGRESS (2:17, 24) | | |

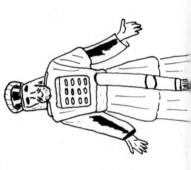

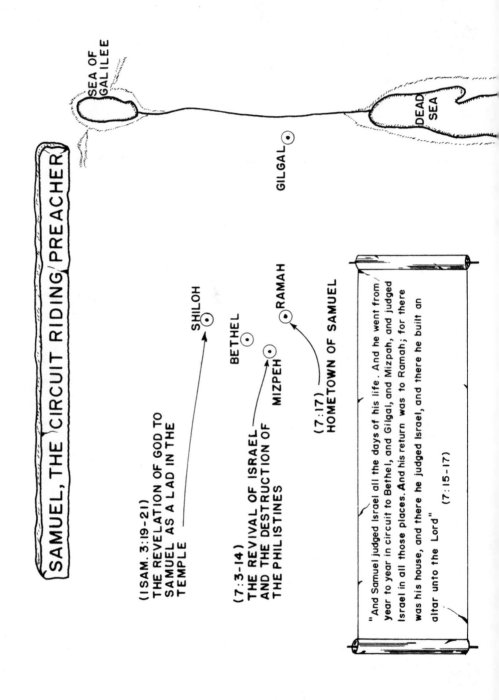

# SAMUEL, THE CIRCUIT RIDING PREACHER

SEA OF GALILEE

DEAD SEA

GILGAL ⊙

SHILOH ⊙

(I SAM. 3:19-21)
THE REVELATION OF GOD TO
SAMUEL AS A LAD IN THE
TEMPLE

BETHEL ⊙

MIZPEH ⊙

RAMAH ⊙

(7:3-14)
THE REVIVAL OF ISRAEL
AND THE DESTRUCTION OF
THE PHILISTINES

(7:17)
HOMETOWN OF SAMUEL

"And Samuel judged Israel all the days of his life. And he went from year to year in circuit to Bethel, and Gilgal, and Mizpah, and judged Israel in all those places. And his return was to Ramah; for there was his house, and there he judged Israel, and there he built an altar unto the Lord"

(7:15-17)

106

THE

# UNITED

# KINGDOM STAGE

FIRST SAMUEL 8-31          SECOND SAMUEL

FIRST KINGS I-II          I CHRONICLES

II CHRONICLES I-9          PSALMS

PROVERBS          ECCLESIASTES

SONG OF SOLOMON

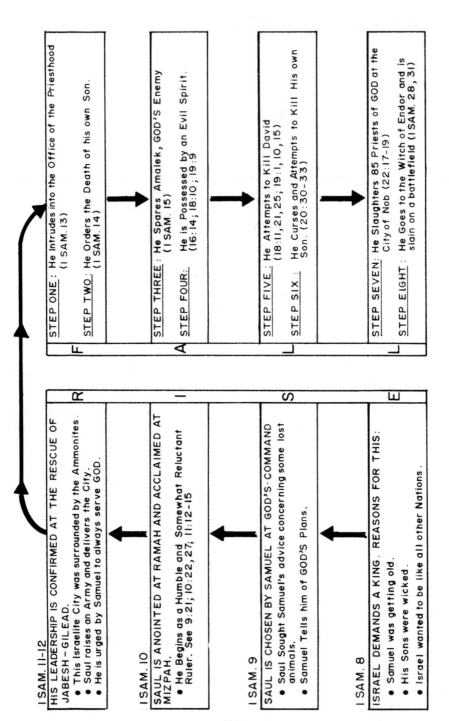

**I SAM. 11-12**

**HIS LEADERSHIP IS CONFIRMED AT THE RESCUE OF JABESH-GILEAD.**
- This Israelite City was surrounded by the Ammonites.
- Saul raises an Army and delivers the City.
- He is urged by Samuel to always serve GOD.

**I SAM. 10**

**SAUL IS ANOINTED AT RAMAH AND ACCLAIMED AT MIZPAH.**
- He Begins as a Humble and Somewhat Reluctant Ruler. See 9:21; 10:22, 27; 11:12-15

**I SAM. 9**

**SAUL IS CHOSEN BY SAMUEL AT GOD'S·COMMAND**
- Saul Sought Samuel's advice concerning some lost animals.
- Samuel Tells him of GOD'S Plans.

**I SAM. 8**

**ISRAEL DEMANDS A KING. REASONS FOR THIS:**
- Samuel was getting old.
- His Sons were wicked.
- Israel wanted to be like all other Nations.

**STEP ONE :** He Intrudes into the Office of the Priesthood (I SAM. 13)

**STEP TWO :** He Orders the Death of his own Son. (I SAM. 14)

**STEP THREE :** He Spares Amalek, GOD'S Enemy (I SAM. 15)

**STEP FOUR:** He is Possessed by an Evil Spirit. (16:14; 18:10; 19:9

**STEP FIVE :** He Attempts to Kill David (18:11, 21, 25; 19:1, 10, 15)

**STEP SIX :** He Curses and Attempts to Kill His own Son. (20:30-33)

**STEP SEVEN:** He Slaughters 85 Priests of GOD at the City of Nob (22:17-19)

**STEP EIGHT :** He Goes to the Witch of Endor and is slain on a battlefield (I SAM. 28, 31)

R I S E

F A L L

# THE RISE AND FALL OF KING SAUL

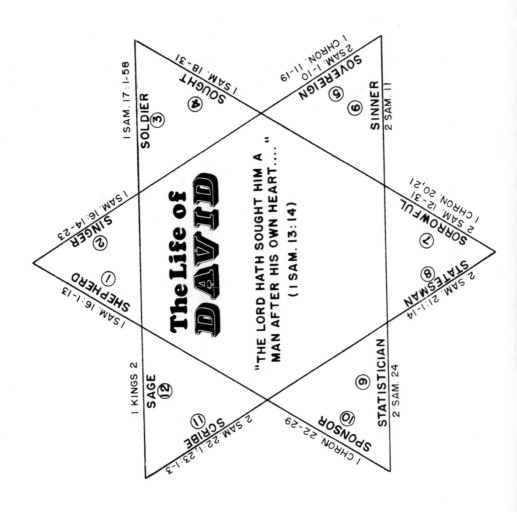

The Life of DAVID

"THE LORD HATH SOUGHT HIM A MAN AFTER HIS OWN HEART...."

(1 SAM. 13:14)

① SHEPHERD — 1 SAM. 16:1-13
② SINGER — 1 SAM. 16:14-23
③ SOLDIER — 1 SAM. 17:1-58
④ SOUGHT — 1 SAM. 18-31
⑤ SOVEREIGN — 2 SAM. 1-10 / 1 CHRON. 11-19
⑥ SINNER — 2 SAM. 11
⑦ SORROWFUL — 2 SAM. 12-31 / 1 CHRON. 20,21
⑧ STATESMAN — 2 SAM. 2:1-14
⑨ STATISTICIAN — 2 SAM. 24
⑩ SPONSOR — 1 CHRON. 22-29
⑪ SCRIBE — 2 SAM. 22:1,23:1-3
⑫ SAGE — 1 KINGS 2

1. DAVID, THE 8th SON OF JESSE IS FETCHED FROM A SHEEP FIELD NEAR BETHLEHEM AND ANOINTED BY SAMUEL. (I SAM. 16:1-12)

2. THE SPIRIT OF GOD COMES UPON DAVID. (16:13)

1. KING SAUL IS TROUBLED BY AN EVIL SPIRIT.

2. DAVID'S BEAUTIFUL MUSIC ON THE HARP HELPS SOOTHE THE TROUBLED KING. (I SAM. 16:14-25)

1. A GIANT PHILISTINE WARRIOR NAMED GOLIATH HAD DEFIED THE ARMIES OF ISRAEL FOR 40 DAYS (17:16)

2. WITH BUT A SLING AND A STONE DAVID KILLS THIS MIGHTY SOLDIER. (17:49)

110

THE
SOUGHT
4

1. HE BEGINS HIS LIFE LONG FELLOWSHIP WITH JONATHAN. (I SAM. 18:1-4, 20:41, 42; 23:16-18)

2. HIS GROWING POPULARITY INCURS SAUL'S INSANE JEALOUSY, WHO ATTEMPTS TO DO HIM IN BY:
   A. JONATHAN (COMPARE 18:5 WITH 18:13)
   B. PRIVATE ATTEMPTS ON HIS LIFE (18:11, 21, 25; 19:1, 10, 15)
   C. TRICKERY (18:25-27)
   D. OPENLY HUNTING HIM AS A WILD ANIMAL (23:15, 26; 24:2, 26:2, 17-20)

3. HE MARRIES MICHAL, THE FIRST OF MANY WIVES (18:27)

4. HE FLEES TO THE CITY OF NOB AND IN DESPERATION LIES TO THE HIGH PRIEST THERE (21:1-9)

5. HE THEN TRAVELS TO THE PHILISTINE CITY OF GATH AND FAKES INSANITY (21:10-15)

6. HE BEGINS GATHERING HIS ARMY OF "SPIRITUAL OUTLAWS." (22:1, 2; 23:13)

7. HE GOES TO MOAB BUT IS ORDERED TO JUDAH BY GOD (22:3-5)

8. HE SPARES THE LIFE OF SAUL ON TWO OCCASIONS:
   A. IN A CAVE IN EN-GEDI (24:1-15)
   B. IN A WILDERNESS IN ZIPH (26:1-16)

9. HE MARRIES HIS SECOND WIFE, A WIDOW NAMED ABIGAIL (25:1-42)

10. AGAIN HE BACKSLIDES AND SETTLES IN THE PHILISTINE CITY OF ZIKLAG (27:1-6)

THE
SOVEREIGN
5

1. UPON THE DEATH OF SAUL BY GOD'S COMMAND HE COMES TO HEBRON AND IS ANOINTED BY THE MEN OF JUDAH AS THEIR KING (2 SAM. 2:1-4)

2. AFTER A 7 YEAR WAR, DAVID IS SUCCESSFUL OVER THE HOUSE OF SAUL AND IS ANOINTED AT HEBRON BY ALL 12 TRIBES (2 SAM. 3-5)

3. HE CAPTURES THE CITY OF JERUSALEM AND MAKES IT HIS NEW CAPITAL (2 SAM. 5:6-10)

4. HE THEN BRINGS THE ARK OF THE COVENANT INTO JERUSALEM (2 SAM. 6:1-19; I CHRON. 15-16)

5. HE DESIRES TO BUILD A TEMPLE FOR GOD, BUT IS NOT ALLOWED TO DO SO. (2 SAM. 7: 17 ; I CHRON. 17:4)

6. HE NOW RECEIVES THE ALL-IMPORTANT DAVIDIC COVENANT FROM GOD (2 SAM. 7:8-17; I CHRON. 17:7-15)
THIS COVENANT IN ESSENCE PREDICTED THE MILLENNIAL REIGN OF CHRIST, THE SEED OF DAVID, UPON THE EARTH SOMEDAY.

7. HE SEEKS OUT AND SHOWS KINDNESS TO MEPHIBOSHETH, JONATHAN'S LAME SON. (2 SAM. 9:1-13)

THE
SINNER
6

1. DAVID COMMITS ADULTERY WITH BATH-SHEBA.

2. HE THAN ARRANGES TO HAVE HER HUSBAND URIAH KILLED ON A BATTLE FIELD. (2 SAM. 11)

THE
SORROWFUL
7

1. NATHAN THE PROPHET CONFRONTS DAVID ABOUT THIS, AND THE KING CONFESSES. (2 SAM. 12:1-12; PSALMS 32,51)

2. GOD FORGIVES HIM, BUT DETERMINES DAVID WOULD PAY BACK FOUR-FOLD. (COMPARE 12:5-6 WITH 12:9-12) THIS WOULD INVOLVE:
   A. THE DEATH OF HIS INFANT SON (12:18)
   B. THE RAPE OF TAMAR, HIS DAUGHTER, BY AMNON, HIS SON.(13:14)
   C. THE MURDER OF AMNON BY HIS HALF-BROTHER (AND DAVID'S SON) ABSALOM (13:29)
   D. THE REBELLION OF ABSALOM AGAINST HIS FATHER'S OWN THRONE (15-18)

THE
STATESMAN
8

1. GOD HAD SENT A THREE-YEAR PLAGUE UPON ISRAEL TO PUNISH THEM FOR SAUL'S PAST SINS AGAINST THE NATION GIBEON.

2. HE STAYS THE PLAGUE BY NEGOTIATING WITH THE GIBEONITES WHO AGREE JUSTICE COULD ONLY BE SERVED BY PERMITTING THEM TO EXECUTE SEVEN OF SAUL'S GUILTY SONS. (2 SAM. 21:1-14)

THE
STATISTICIAN
9

1. HE SUCCUMBS TO THE TEMPTATION OF SATAN AND NUMBERS ISRAEL (1 CHRON. 21:1-6)

2. A DIVINE PLAGUE OCCURS, WHICH IS FINALLY STOPPED BY DAVID AS HE PLEADS WITH THE DEATH ANGEL (2 SAM. 24:15-25; 1 CHRON. 21:18-30)

THE
SPONSOR
10

1. HE PRESIDES OVER A GREAT DEDICATORY SERVICE FOR THE FUTURE TEMPLE (1 CHRON. 22: 5, 9, 10)
2. HE HIMSELF CONTRIBUTES MILLIONS OF DOLLARS AND HELPS RAISE ADDITIONAL MILLIONS (1 CHRON. 29:4,6,7)
3. HE GIVES THE TEMPLE BLUE PRINTS HE RECEIVED FROM GOD TO SOLOMON (28:19)
4. HE THEN OFFERS ONE OF SCRIPTURE'S MOST BEAUTIFUL PRAYERS (29:10-19)

THE
SCRIBE
11

DAVID WRITES OVER HALF OF THE PSALMS IN THE WORD OF GOD.

"THE SPIRIT OF THE LORD SPOKE BY ME, AND HIS WORD WAS IN MY TONGUE." (2 SAM. 23:2) SEE ALSO 23:1-3; 22:1

THE
SAGE
12

ON HIS DEATH BED DAVID EXHORTS SOLOMON TO DO THE FOLLOWING:
1. ACT LIKE A MAN OF GOD (1 KINGS 2:2)
2. BE TRUE TO THE WORD OF GOD (2:3)
3. RELY ON THE PROMISES OF GOD (2:4)
4. EXECUTE THE JUDGMENT OF GOD (2:5 )

# SOLOMON

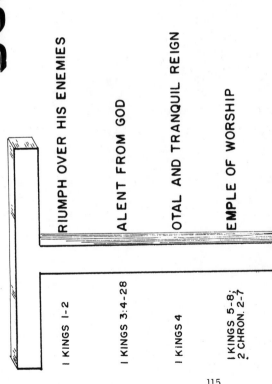

**TRIUMPH OVER HIS ENEMIES**
I KINGS 1-2
- ADONIJAH • JOAB
- ABIATHAR • SHIMEI

**TALENT FROM GOD**
I KINGS 3:4-28
- THE TALENT - WISDOM
- THE TEST - A BABY AND A SWORD

**TOTAL AND TRANQUIL REIGN**
I KINGS 4
- A BEAUTIFUL TYPE OF CHRIST'S MILLENNIAL RULE

**TEMPLE OF WORSHIP**
I KINGS 5-8;
2 CHRON. 2-7
- TWICE THE SIZE OF THE TABERNACLE.
- 7 YEARS IN CONSTRUCTION

**TREASURY OF RICHES**
4:26; 9:17, 26-28;
10:22, 26; 11:3
- MUCH GOLD
- MANY HORSES, CHARIOTS
- A FLEET OF SHIPS

**TESTIMONY THROUGHOUT LAND**
4:29-34; 10:1-13
- AS TESTIFIED BY THE QUEEN OF SHEBA

**TRANSGRESSIONS AGAINST GOD**
I KINGS 11
- HE DISOBEYED DEUT. 17:14-17 AND ACCUMULATED :
  - MUCH GOLD
  - MANY WIVES
  - MANY HORSES

# SOLOMON'S TEMPLE

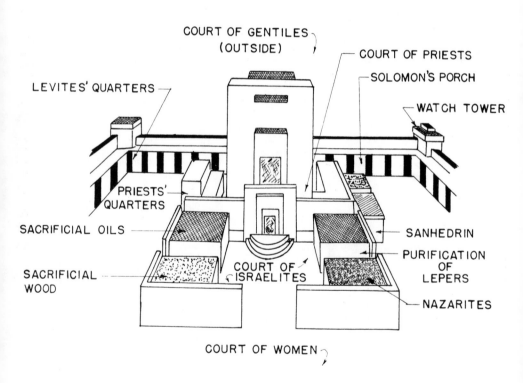

COURT OF GENTILES
(OUTSIDE)

COURT OF PRIESTS

SOLOMON'S PORCH

LEVITES' QUARTERS

WATCH TOWER

PRIESTS' QUARTERS

SACRIFICIAL OILS

SANHEDRIN

SACRIFICIAL WOOD

COURT OF ISRAELITES

PURIFICATION OF LEPERS

NAZARITES

COURT OF WOMEN

# the book of PSALMS

## BY BOOK DIVISION

| CHAPTERS | HOW SIMILAR TO PENTATEUCH |
| --- | --- |
| 1-41 | KEY WORD IS MAN (CORRESPONDS TO GENESIS) |
| 42-72 | KEY WORD IS DELIVERANCE (CORRESPONDS TO EXODUS) |
| 73-89 | KEY WORD IS SANCTUARY (CORRESPONDS TO LEVITICUS) |
| 90-106 | KEY WORDS ARE WANDERING UNREST (CORRESPONDS TO NUMBERS) |
| 107-150 | KEY WORD IS WORD OF GOD (CORRESPONDS TO DEUTERONOMY) |

## BY SUBJECT MATTER

| SUBJECT | PSALMS |
| --- | --- |
| PENITENTIAL | 6,32,38,51,102,130,143 |
| IMPRECATORY | 35,55,58,59,69,83,109,137,140 |
| DEGREE OR ASCENT | 120-134 |
| HALLELUJAH | 113-118 |
| HISTORICAL | 78,105,106 |
| ACROSTIC | 9,10,25,34,37,111,112,119,145 |
| MESSIANIC | 16,22,24,31,34,40,41,45,55,68,69,89, 102,109,110,118,129 |

## BY AUTHORSHIP

| AUTHOR | PSALMS |
| --- | --- |
| DAVID:77 | o SHEPHERD PSALMS - 8,19,23,29,144 |
| | o SINNER PSALMS - 32,51,38 |
| | o SUFFERING PSALMS - 3,4,5,6,7,11,12,13, 14,17,22,25,26,27,28,31,34,35,39,40, 41,53,54,55,56,57,58,59,61,62,63,64, 69,70,86,109,140,141,142,143 |
| | o SATISFIED PSALMS - 2,9,15,16,18,20,21, 24,30,36,37,52,60,65,68,72,95,101,103, 105,108,110,122,124,131,133,138,139,145 |
| KORAH:10 | 42,44,45,46,47,48,49,84,85,87 |
| ASAPH:12 | 50,73,74,75,76,77,78,79,80,81,82,83 |
| HEMAN:1 | 88 |
| ETHAN:1 | 89 |
| SOLOMON:1 | 127 |
| MOSES:1 | 90 |
| HEZEKIAH:10 | 120,121,123,125,126,128,129,130,132,134 |
| ANONYMOUS 37 | 1,10,33,43,66,67,71,91,92,93,94,96,97, 98,99,100,102,104,106,107,111,112,113, 114,115,116,117,118,119,135,136,137,146,147, 148,149,150 |

| PSALM REFERENCE | FEATURE OF CHRIST DESCRIBED | N.T. FULFILLMENT |
|---|---|---|
| 40:6-10 | HIS OBEDIENCE | HEB. 10:5-7 |
| 69:9 | HIS ZEAL | JOHN 2:17 |
| 118:22 | HIS REJECTION | MATT. 21:42 |
| 41:9; 55:12-14 | HIS BETRAYAL | MATT. 26:14-16, 21-25 |
| 22:1,6,7,8,16,18; 31:5; 34:20; 69:21; 129:3 | HIS SUFFERINGS | MATT. 27:34,48; LK. 23:46; JN. 19:33-36 |
| 109:2,3 | HIS FALSE WITNESSES | MATT. 26:59-61, 27:39-44 |
| 109:4 | HIS PRAYER FOR HIS ENEMIES | LK. 23:34 |
| 16:10 | HIS RESURRECTION | ACTS 13:35 |
| 68:18 | HIS ASCENSION | EPH. 4:8 |
| 24:7-8 | HIS TRIUMPHAL ENTRY INTO GLORY | PHIL. 2:9-11 |
| 110:4 | HIS HIGH PRIESTLY WORK | HEB. 5-7 |
| 45:2,6,8,13,15 | HIS MARRIAGE TO THE CHURCH | REV. 19:7-10 |
| 110:1,6 | HIS DESTRUCTION OF THE HEATHEN | REV. 6-19 |
| 89:27; 102:16-21; 72:17 | HIS MILLENNIAL REIGN | MATT. 23:39; REV. 11:15 |

# Messianic Psalms

# SUGGESTED NAMES FOR SOME OF THE PSALMS

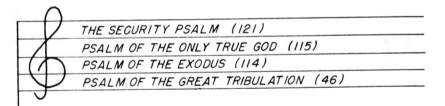

PSALM OF THE GODLY MAN  (1)

PSALMS OF CREATION  (8,104)

THE GOOD SHEPHERD PSALM (22)

THE GREAT SHEPHERD PSALM (23)

THE CHIEF SHEPHERD PSALM (24)

THE UNITY PSALM (133)

PSALMS OF JERUSALEM (48, 122, 126, 132, 137)

PSALMS ABOUT THE FAMILY (127, 128)

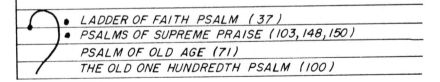

THE SECURITY PSALM  (121)

PSALM OF THE ONLY TRUE GOD  (115)

PSALM OF THE EXODUS (114)

PSALM OF THE GREAT TRIBULATION  (46)

LADDER OF FAITH PSALM  (37)

PSALMS OF SUPREME PRAISE (103, 148, 150)

PSALM OF OLD AGE (71)

THE OLD ONE HUNDREDTH PSALM (100)

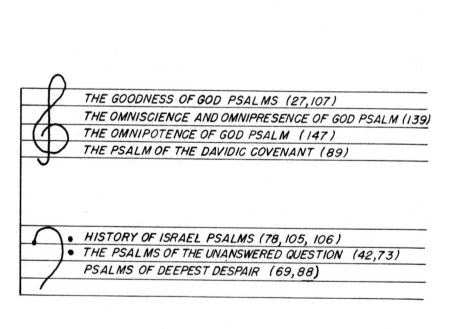

PSALM OF DEATH (90)
PSALM OF LIFE (91)
THE DELIVERANCE PSALMS (31,116)
THE HOUSE OF GOD PSALM (84)

THE WEALTH OF GOD PSALM (50)
THE WORD OF GOD PSALMS (19,119)
THE VOICE OF GOD PSALM (29)
THE MERCY OF GOD PSALM (136)

THE GOODNESS OF GOD PSALMS (27,107)
THE OMNISCIENCE AND OMNIPRESENCE OF GOD PSALM (139)
THE OMNIPOTENCE OF GOD PSALM (147)
THE PSALM OF THE DAVIDIC COVENANT (89)

HISTORY OF ISRAEL PSALMS (78,105,106)
THE PSALMS OF THE UNANSWERED QUESTION (42,73)
PSALMS OF DEEPEST DESPAIR (69,88)

# the book of PROVERBS

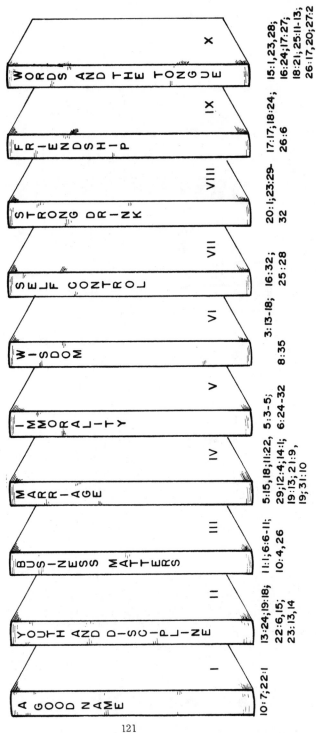

| | | Theme | References |
|---|---|---|---|
| X | WORDS AND THE TONGUE | | 15:1,23,28; 16:24,17:27; 18:21; 25:11-13; 26:17,20;27:2 |
| IX | FRIENDSHIP | | 17:17,18:24; 26:6 |
| VIII | STRONG DRINK | | 20:1;23:29-32 |
| VII | SELF CONTROL | | 16:32; 25:28 |
| VI | WISDOM | | 3:13-18; 8:35 |
| V | IMMORALITY | | 5:3-5; 6:24-32 |
| IV | MARRIAGE | | 5:15,18;11:22, 29;12:4,14:1; 19;13, 21:9, 19;31:10 |
| III | BUSINESS MATTERS | | 11:1; 6:6-11; 10:4,26 |
| II | YOUTH AND DISCIPLINE | | 13:24;19:18; 22:6,15; 23:13,14 |
| I | A GOOD NAME | | 10:7,22:1 |

**Ten Timely Themes**

121

# CLASSICAL PASSAGES

*"A WORD SPOKEN IN DUE SEASON, HOW GOOD IS IT!" (15:23)*

| CHAPTER | VERSES |
|---------|--------|
| 1 | 24-28 |
| 3 | 5,6,9,10-12,19-26 |
| 6 | 16-19 |
| 8 | 22-31 |
| 11 | 30 |
| 14 | 12,34 |
| 16 | 3,7,18 |
| 18 | 10 |
| 24 | 16,17,28,29 |
| 25 | 19-22 |
| 27 | 1 |
| 28 | 13 |
| 29 | 1,18 |
| 30 | 4-9,11-14 |
| 31 | 10-12,28,30 |

## the book of PROVERBS

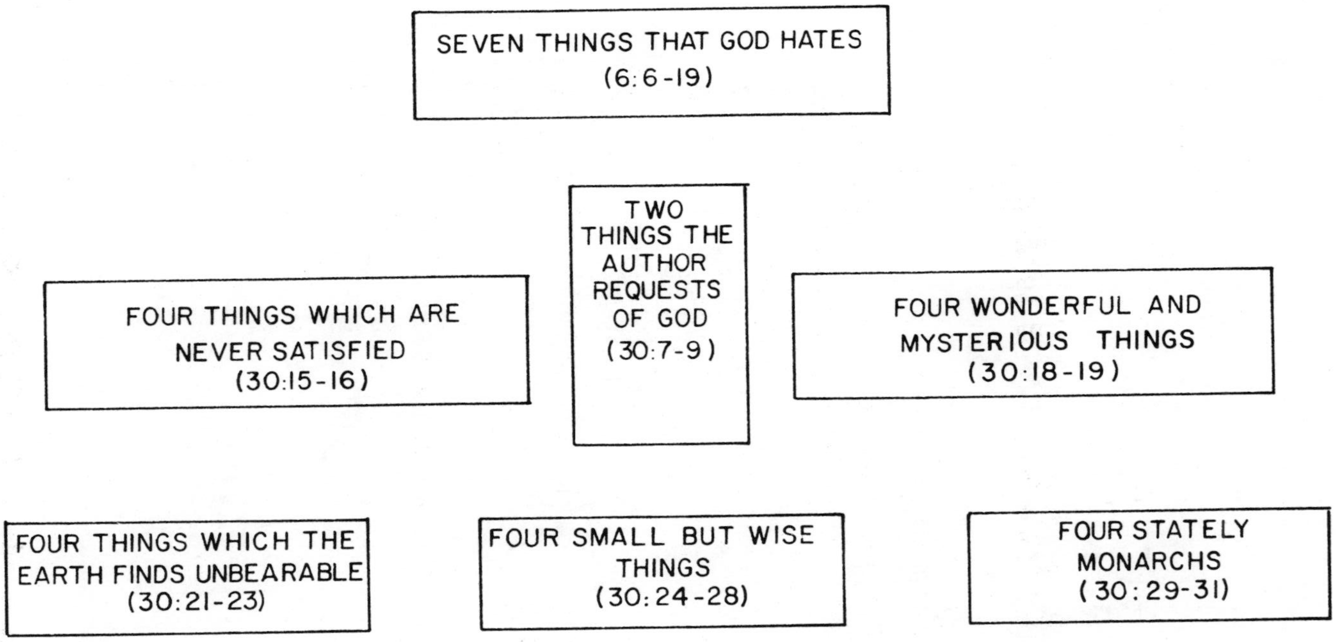

SEVEN THINGS THAT GOD HATES
(6:6-19)

TWO
THINGS THE
AUTHOR
REQUESTS
OF GOD
(30:7-9)

FOUR WONDERFUL AND
MYSTERIOUS THINGS
(30:18-19)

FOUR STATELY
MONARCHS
(30:29-31)

FOUR THINGS WHICH ARE
NEVER SATISFIED
(30:15-16)

FOUR SMALL BUT WISE
THINGS
(30:24-28)

FOUR THINGS WHICH THE
EARTH FINDS UNBEARABLE
(30:21-23)

# A GALLERY OF GROUPS

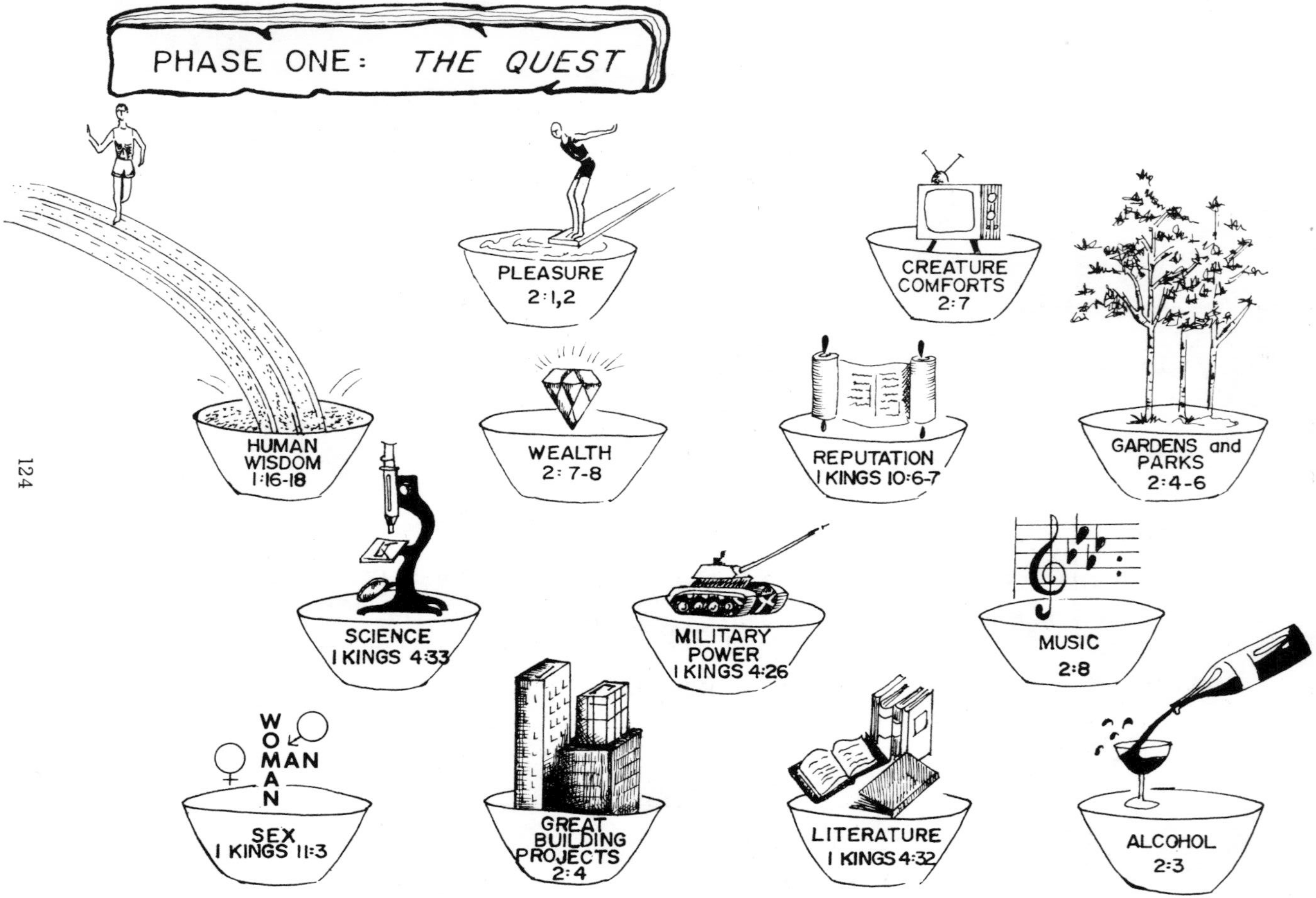

THE BOOK OF ECCLESIASTES

PHASE ONE : THE QUEST

HUMAN WISDOM 1:16-18

SCIENCE I KINGS 4:33

SEX I KINGS 11:3

WOMAN

PLEASURE 2:1,2

WEALTH 2:7-8

GREAT BUILDING PROJECTS 2:4

MILITARY POWER I KINGS 4:26

LITERATURE I KINGS 4:32

CREATURE COMFORTS 2:7

REPUTATION I KINGS 10:6-7

GARDENS and PARKS 2:4-6

MUSIC 2:8

ALCOHOL 2:3

124

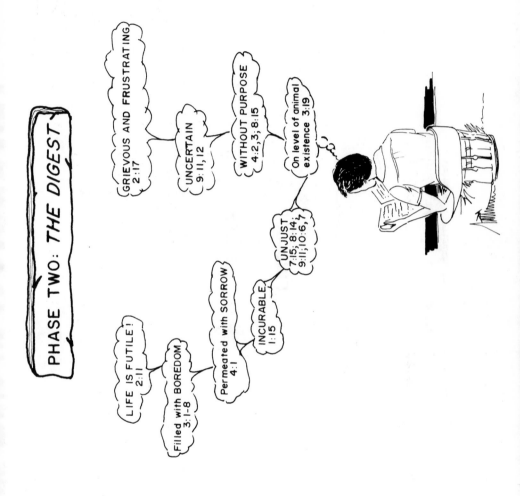

PHASE TWO: *THE DIGEST*

GRIEVOUS AND FRUSTRATING 2:17

UNCERTAIN 9:11,12

WITHOUT PURPOSE 4:2,3; 8:15

On level of animal existence 3:19

UNJUST 7:15; 8:14; 9:11;10:6,7

INCURABLE 1:15

LIFE IS FUTILE! 2:11

Filled with BOREDOM 3:1-8

Permeated with SORROW 4:1

PHASE THREE: *THE BEST*

FIND GOD EARLY IN YOUR LIFE !
(11:9-10; 12:1-2)

FEAR GOD THROUGHOUT YOUR LIFE !
(12:1,2,10,11-14)

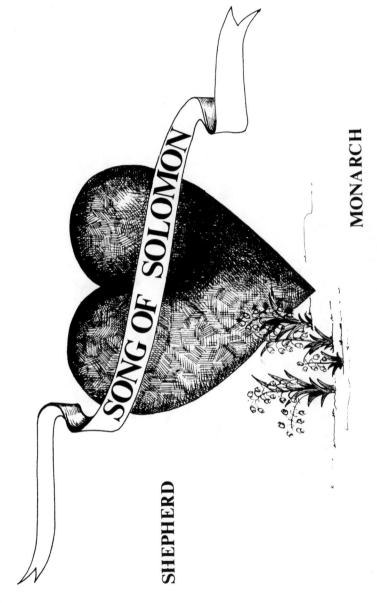

SHULAMITE

MONARCH

SONG OF SOLOMON

SHEPHERD

# ACT ONE

## The Shulamite Cinderella

**PLOT ACTION:**

A family of sharecroppers work in a vineyard in the little town of SHUNAM, 50 miles north of JERUSALEM. The oldest daughter is the CINDERELLA of the story, having great natural beauty, but subject to burdensome labor in the vineyard by her brothers.

# The Mysterious Shepherd

## PLOT ACTION:

One day a handsome stranger visits the vineyard and wins the heart of the SHULAMITE girl. Unknown to her, he was really SOLOMON, disguised as a lowly shepherd.

He soon leaves her, but promises to return. During his absence she has two dreams about him. In both dreams she sees herself married to him, but slow to respond to his affection to her.

# ACT TWO

129

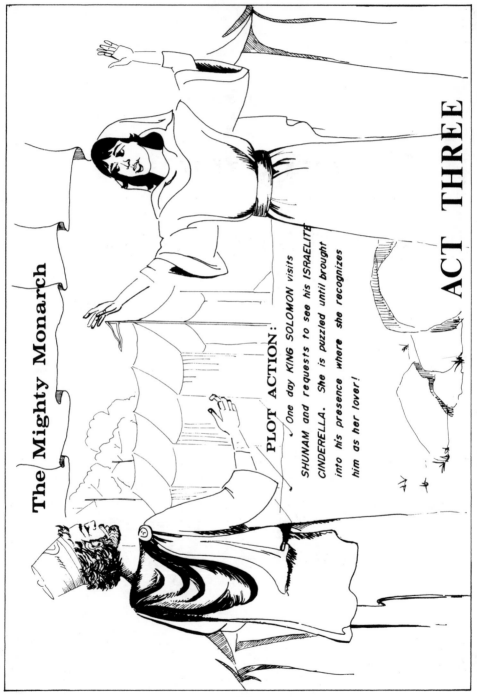

The Mighty Monarch

ACT THREE

PLOT ACTION:
One day KING SOLOMON visits SHUNAM and requests to see his ISRAELITE CINDERELLA. She is puzzled until brought into his presence where she recognizes him as her lover!

THE

# CHAOTIC

# KINGDOM STAGE

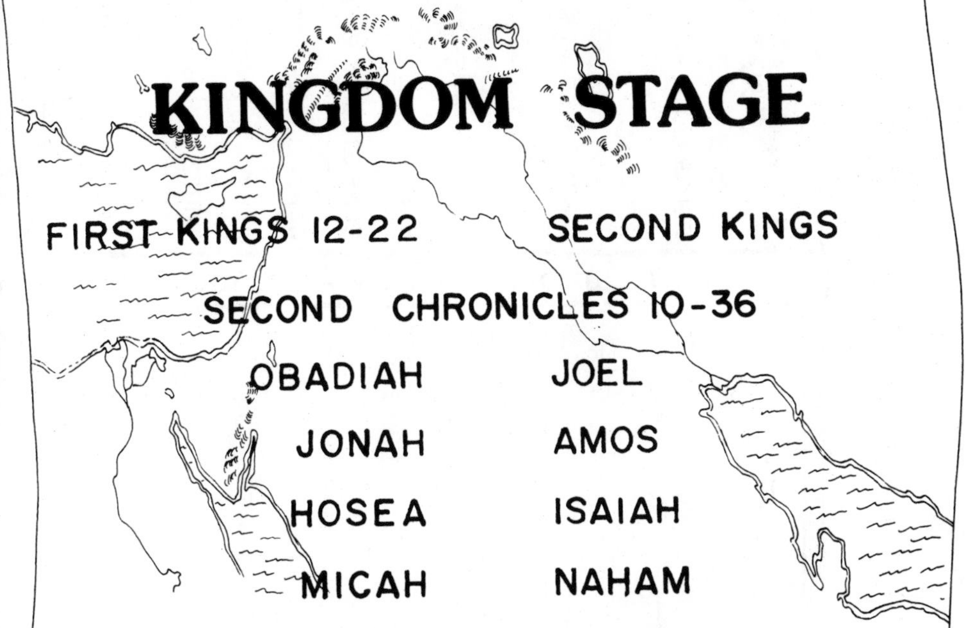

FIRST KINGS 12-22          SECOND KINGS

SECOND   CHRONICLES 10-36

OBADIAH          JOEL

JONAH          AMOS

HOSEA          ISAIAH

MICAH          NAHAM

ZEPHANIAH          JEREMIAH

HABAKKUK          LAMENTATIONS

# A TALE OF TWO KINGDOMS

| NORTHERN KINGDOM | | SOUTHERN KINGDOM |
|---|---|---|
| REFERRED TO AS ISRAEL AND EPHRAIM | A | REFERRED TO AS JUDAH |
| BEGAN IN 931 B.C. | T | BEGAN IN 931 B.C. |
| FIRST RULER WAS JEROBOAM | A | FIRST RULER WAS REHOBOAM |
| LAST RULER WAS HOSHEA | E | LAST RULER WAS ZEDEKIAH |
| TOTAL NUMBER OF RULERS - 19 | O | TOTAL NUMBER OF RULERS - 20 |
| NOT ONE WAS SAVED | F | 8 WERE SAVED |
| CONSISTED OF 10 TRIBES | T | CONSISTED OF 2 TRIBES |
| CAPITAL WAS SAMARIA | W | CAPITAL WAS JERUSALEM |
| CAPTURED BY THE ASSYRIANS IN 721 B.C. | O | CAPTURED BY THE BABYLONIANS IN 606 B.C. |
| NO RETURN FROM CAPTIVITY | K I N G D | THREE SEPARATE RETURNS FROM CAPTIVITY |
| LASTED 210 YRS. 931-721 B.C. | O M S | LASTED 325 YRS. 931-606 - B.C. |

# THE CHAOTIC KINGDOM KINGS

| | | | |
|---|---|---|---|
| REHOBOAM | JOTHAM | JEROBOAM | JEHOAHAZ |
| ABIJAM | AHAZ | NADAB | JEHOASH |
| ASA | HEZEKIAH | BAASHA | JEROBOAM II |
| JEHOSHAPHAT | MANASSEH | ELAH | ZECHARIAH |
| JEHORAM | AMON | ZIMRI | SHALLUM |
| AHAZIAH | JOSIAH | OMRI | MENAHEM |
| ATHALIAH | JEHOAHAZ | AHAB | PEKAHIAH |
| JOASH | JEHOIAKIM | AHAZIAH | PEKAH |
| AMAZIAH | JEHOIACHIN | JEHORAM | HOSHEA |
| UZZIAH | ZEDEKIAH | JEHU | |

# —NORTHERN RULERS—

## I

JEROBOAM

| DATES | DURATION | SCRIPTURE |
|-------|----------|-----------|
| 931-909 | 22 YRS. | I KINGS 11:26-14:20; 2 CHRON. 9:29-13:22 |

1. SERVED AS A CABINET MEMBER UNDER SOLOMON, BUT FLED TO EGYPT TO ESCAPE THE KING'S WRATH.

2. LED THE REVOLT OF THE 10 TRIBES AT SHECHEM.

3. HIS FALSE RELIGION CAUSED ISRAEL TO SIN.

4. HIS PAGAN ALTAR WAS DESTROYED, HIS ARM PARALYZED, AND HIS SON STRICKEN BY GOD DUE TO HIS SIN.

5. WAS DEFEATED IN BATTLE BY ABIJAM, THE SECOND KING OF THE SOUTH.

6. WAS STRICKEN WITH A PLAGUE FROM GOD AND DIED.

## II

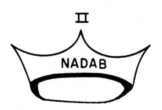

NADAB

| DATES | DURATION | SCRIPTURE |
|-------|----------|-----------|
| 910-908 | 2 YRS | I KINGS 15:25-28 |

1. WAS THE SON OF JEROBOAM

2. WAS ASSASSINATED BY A REBEL NAMED BAASHA

**III**

**BAASHA**

| DATES | DURATION | SCRIPTURE |
|-------|----------|-----------|
| 909-885 | 24 YRS. | I KINGS 15:27-16:7; 2 CHRON. 16:1-6 |

1. KILLED NADAB AND THUS FULFILLED AHIJAH THE PROPHET'S PREDICTION. COMPARE I KINGS 14:4 WITH 15:29.
2. FOUGHT WITH ASA (3rd KING OF SOUTH) AND BUILT A BERLIN WALL TO CUT OFF TRADE TO JERUSALEM.
3. HIS SEED WAS PREDICTED TO SUFFER THE SAME JUDGMENT AS THAT OF JEROBOAM.

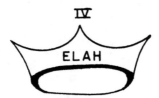

**IV**

**ELAH**

| DATES | DURATION | SCRIPTURE |
|-------|----------|-----------|
| 885-883 | 2 YRS. | I KINGS 16:6-14 |

1. WAS THE SON OF BAASHA
2. WAS ASSASSINATED BY A SOLDIER REBEL WHILE DRUNK.

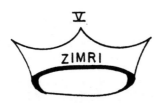

**V**

**ZIMRI**

| DATES | DURATION | SCRIPTURE |
|-------|----------|-----------|
| 885 | 7 DAYS | I KINGS 16:9-20 |

1. FULFILLED PROPHECY BY SLAUGHTERING BAASHA'S SEED.
2. WAS TRAPPED BY REBEL SOLDIERS IN HIS OWN PALACE, RESULTING IN A FIERY-SUICIDAL DEATH.

135

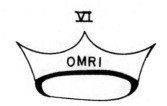

**VI**

OMRI

| DATES | DURATION | SCRIPTURE |
|-------|----------|-----------|
| 885-873 | 12 YRS. | I KINGS 16:15-28 |

1. MADE SAMARIA THE NORTHERN CAPITAL.
2. MOST POWERFUL KING UP TO HIS TIME.
3. ARRANGED THE MARRIAGE OF HIS SON AHAB TO JEZEBEL.

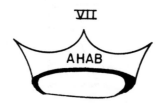

**VII**

AHAB

| DATES | DURATION | SCRIPTURE |
|-------|----------|-----------|
| 874-852 | 22 YRS. | I KINGS 16:28-22:40; 2 CHRON. 18:1-34 |

1. HE MARRIED JEZEBEL.

2. HIS BAAL WORSHIPPING PRACTICES CAUSED A GREAT FAMINE TO FALL UPON THE LAND.

3. HE WAS ALLOWED TO DEFEAT THE SYRIANS ON TWO OCCASIONS TO PROVE A POINT.

4. HE TRICKED GODLY KING JEHOSHAPHAT (4th JUDEAN KING) INTO A TWO-FOLD COMPROMISE.
   A. A MATRIMONIAL ALLIANCE, WHEREBY HIS WICKED DAUGHTER ATHALIAH WAS GIVEN TO JORAM, SON OF JEHOSHAPHAT
   B. A MILITARY ALLIANCE, WHEREBY JEHOSHAPHAT AND AHAB WENT TO WAR AGAINST SYRIA.

5. HIS DEATH FOR HIS MANY SINS IS PREDICTED BY 3 PROPHETS.
   A. AN UNKNOWN PROPHET (I KINGS 20:42)
   B. ELIJAH (I KINGS 21:19)
   C. MICAIAH (I KINGS 22:17,28)

6. THE DEATH OF JEZEBEL HIS WIFE IS PREDICTED ALSO BY ELIJAH.

7. HE EXPERIENCED A BRIEF (BUT TEMPORARY) FOX-HOLE TYPE RELIGION (I KINGS 21:29)

8. HE IS KILLED IN A BATTLE WITH SYRIA

## VIII AHAZIAH

| DATES | DURATION | SCRIPTURE |
|-------|----------|-----------|
| 853-851 | 2 YRS. | I KINGS 22:40 - 2 KINGS 1:18; 2 CHRON. 20:35-37 |

1. WAS THE OLDEST SON OF AHAB AND JEZEBEL.
2. PERSUADED JEHOSHAPHAT TO ENTER INTO A SHIP-BUILDING ENTERPRIZE WITH HIM AT EZION-GEBER.
3. SUFFERED A SEVERE (WHICH PROVED FATAL) FALL IN HIS PALACE IN SAMARIA.
4. TURNED TO THE PAGAN GOD BAAL-ZEBUB FOR HEALING.
5. WAS REBUKED FOR THIS BY ELIJAH, WHOM HE UNSUCCESSFULLY ATTEMPTED TO ARREST.

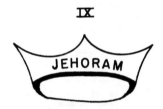

## IX JEHORAM

| DATES | DURATION | SCRIPTURE |
|-------|----------|-----------|
| 852-840 | 12 YRS. | 2 KINGS 3:1-9:25; 2 CHRON. 22:5-7 |

1. WAS THE YOUNGEST SON OF AHAB AND JEZEBEL.
2. PERSUADED JEHOSHAPHAT TO ALLY WITH HIM AGAINST SYRIA.
3. ELISHA THE PROPHET PERFORMS A MIRACLE (FOR JEHOSHAPHAT'S SAKE) WHICH WINS THE BATTLE.
4. ELISHA LATER HELPS JEHORAM BY WARNING HIM OF SEVERAL PLANNED SYRIAN AMBUSHES.
5. ELISHA WOULD HOWEVER, PREVENT HIM FROM SLAUGHTERING SOME SUPER-NATURALLY BLINDED SYRIAN TROOPS.
6. WAS ON THE THRONE WHEN NAAMAN CAME TO BE HEALED OF LEPROSY.
7. WAS ON THE THRONE WHEN GOD USED 4 LEPERS TO SAVE SAMARIA FROM STARVATION.
8. WAS FINALLY MURDERED BY JEHU IN THE VALLEY OF JEZREEL.

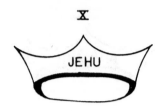

X

JEHU

| DATES | DURATION | SCRIPTURE |
|-------|----------|-----------|
| 841-813 | 28 YRS. | 2 KINGS 9:1-10:36; 2 CHRON. 22:7-12 |

1. WAS ANOINTED BY A MESSENGER FROM ELISHA.

2. WAS KNOWN FOR HIS BLOOD-LETTING. HE EXECUTED:
    A. JUDEAN KING AHAZIAH (NOT TO BE CONFUSED WITH AHAB'S OLDEST SON), GRANDSON OF JEHOSHAPHAT.
    B. NORTHERN KING JEHORAM
    C. JEZEBEL
    D. AHAB'S 70 SONS, RELATIVES, AND FRIENDS.
    E. 42 ROYAL PRINCES OF JUDAH.
    F. THE BAALITE WORSHIPPERS.

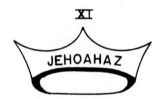

XI

JEHOAHAZ

| DATES | DURATION | SCRIPTURE |
|-------|----------|-----------|
| 814-797 | 17 YRS. | 2 KINGS 13:1-9 |

1. WAS THE SON OF JEHU

2. SAW HIS ARMY ALMOST WIPED OUT BY THE SYRIANS.

3. EXPERIENCED A BRIEF PERIOD OF REMORSE OVER HIS SINS, BUT APPARENTLY NOT GENUINE REPENTANCE

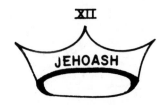

**XII**

**JEHOASH**

| DATES | DURATION | SCRIPTURE |
|---|---|---|
| 798-782 | 16 YRS. | 2 KINGS 13:10-14:16; 2 CHRON. 25:17-24 |

1. VISITED ELISHA ON HIS DEATH BED
2. DEFEATED AMAZIAH (6th KING OF JUDAH) ON THE BATTLE FIELD.
3. RELATED ONE OF THE TWO O.T. FABLES TO RIDICULE THE ARROGANT CLAIMS OF AMAZIAH.
4. PLUNDERED JERUSALEM, TAKING MANY HOSTAGES AND MUCH WEALTH.

**XIII**

**JEROBOAM II**

| DATES | DURATION | SCRIPTURE |
|---|---|---|
| 793-752 | 41 YRS. | 2 KINGS 14:23-29 |

1. RULED LONGER THAN ANY OTHER NORTHERN KING.
2. WAS ONE OF MOST POWERFUL KINGS OF THE NORTH.
3. RECOVERED MUCH OF ISRAEL'S LOST TERRITORY.

**XIV**

**ZECHARIAH**

| DATES | DURATION | SCRIPTURE |
|---|---|---|
| 753 | 6 MONTHS | 2 KINGS 14:29-15:12 |

1. WAS THE GREAT-GREAT GRANDSON OF JEHU, AND 4th RULER IN HIS DYNASTY.
2. WAS MURDERED BY A REBEL NAMED SHALLUM, THUS FULFILLING GOD'S PROPHECY AGAINST JEHU. SEE 2 KINGS 10:30; 14:29; 15:8-12.

## XV

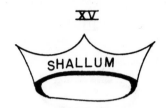

SHALLUM

| DATES | DURATION | SCRIPTURE |
|-------|----------|-----------|
| 752 | I MONTH | 2 KINGS 15:10-15 |

WAS MURDERED BY A CRUEL SOLDIER NAMED MENAHEM

## XVI

MENAHEM

| DATES | DURATION | SCRIPTURE |
|-------|----------|-----------|
| 752-742 | IO YRS. | 2 KINGS 15:14-22 |

1. WAS ONE OF ISRAEL'S MOST BRUTAL DICTATORS.
2. BOUGHT OFF ASSYRIAN KING TIGLATH-PILESER WITH A TWO-MILLION DOLLAR BRIBE.

## XVII

PEKAHIAH

| DATES | DURATION | SCRIPTURE |
|-------|----------|-----------|
| 742-740 | 2 YRS. | 2 KINGS 15:22-26 |

1. WAS SON OF MENAHEM
2. WAS KILLED BY HIS ARMY COMMANDER, PEKAH

PEKAH

| DATES | DURATION | SCRIPTURE |
|-------|----------|-----------|
| 740-732 | 20 YRS. | 2 KINGS 15:27-31; 2 CHRON. 28:5-8 |

1. IT WILL BE NOTED THAT ONLY 8 YEARS ARE IN VIEW HERE (740-732). IT IS THOUGHT THAT THE FIRST 12 YEARS (752-740) WERE SHARED BY A CO-REGENCY ARRANGEMENT WITH BOTH MENAHEM AND PEKAHIAH.

2. HE JOINED SYRIA IN AN UNSUCCESSFUL ATTEMPT TO PUNISH JUDAH FOR THEIR REFUSAL TO TEAM UP WITH THEM AGAINST ASSYRIA.

3. HE SAW ASSYRIA CAPTURE SOME OF ISRAEL'S NORTHERN AND EASTERN CITIES.

4. HE WAS ASSASSINATED BY HOSHEA.

## XIX

HOSHEA

| DATES | DURATION | SCRIPTURE |
|-------|----------|-----------|
| 732-721 | 9 YRS. | 2 KINGS 15:30-17:6 |

1. HE WAS ISRAEL'S FINAL KING.

2. HE JOINED WITH EGYPT IN REBELLING AGAINST ASSYRIA.

3. FOR THIS HE WAS IMPRISONED IN ASSYRIA.

# -SOUTHERN RULERS-

## I

| DATES | DURATION | SCRIPTURE |
|-------|----------|-----------|
| 931-914 | 17 YRS. | I KINGS 11:42-14:31; 2 CHRON. 9:31-12:16 |

1. WAS THE SON OF SOLOMON.
2. HIS STUPIDITY AND TACTLESSNESS SPARKED THE CIVIL WAR.
3. HE HAD 18 WIVES AND 60 CONCUBINES.
4. HIS FAVORITE WIFE WAS MAACHAH, THE EVIL DAUGHTER OF ABSALOM.
5. HE SEES HIS CAPITOL JERUSALEM INVADED BY SHISHAK, PHARAOH OF EGYPT.

## II

| DATES | DURATION | SCRIPTURE |
|-------|----------|-----------|
| 914-911 | 3 YRS. | I KINGS 14:31-15:8; 2 CHRON. 13:1-22 |

1. HE DEFEATED (BY SUPERNATURAL INTERVENTION) THE NORTHERN KING JEROBOAM ON THE BATTLE FIELD.
2. IN SPITE OF GOD'S HELP, HE DEGENERATED INTO A WICKED KING.

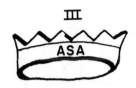

**III**

ASA

| DATES | DURATION | SCRIPTURE |
|-------|----------|-----------|
| 911-870 | 41 YRS | I KINGS 15:8-14; 2 CHRON. 14:1-16:14 |

1. WAS JUDAH'S FIRST SAVED KING.

2. LED JUDAH IN A REVIVAL.

3. WAS A GREAT BUILDER.

4. SAW GOD ANSWER HIS PRAYER BY DELIVERING JERUSALEM FROM A MASSIVE ETHIOPIAN ATTACK (2 CHRON. 14:11)

5. HE DEPOSED MAACAH (HIS GRANDMOTHER) BECAUSE OF HER IDOLATRY.

6. HE LATER BACKSLID AND THREW A PROPHET IN PRISON WHO HAD REBUKED HIS SIN.

7. HE DIED WITH A FOOT DISEASE, WHICH PROBLEM HE REFUSED TO TAKE TO GOD.

**IV**

JEHOSHAPHAT

| DATES | DURATION | SCRIPTURE |
|-------|----------|-----------|
| 873-848 | 25 YRS. | I KINGS 22:41-50; 2 CHRON. 17:1-20:37 |

1. HE INSTITUTED A NATIONAL RELIGIOUS EDUCATION PROGRAM BY SENDING OUT TEACHERS TO INSTRUCT IN THE WORD OF GOD.

2. HE LATER MARRED HIS TESTIMONY BY COMPROMISING WITH THREE UNGODLY NORTHERN KINGS.
   A. MATRIMONIAL ALLIANCE WITH AHAB. JORAM MARRIES ATHALIAH.
   B. MILITARY ALLIANCE WITH AHAB AGAINST SYRIA.
   C. TRADING ALLIANCE WITH AHAZIAH, AHAB'S OLDEST SON.
   D. MILITARY ALLIANCE WITH JEHORAM, AHAB'S YOUNGEST SON.

3. HE APPOINTED A RELIGIOUS DIRECTOR AND A CIVIL DIRECTOR, THUS RECOGNIZING THE SEPARATION OF CHURCH AND STATE.

4. WHEN JERUSALEM IS THREATENED BY A MASSIVE MOABITE INVASION GOD HEARS HIS PRAYER AND SUPERNATURALLY INTERVENES.

## V — JORAM

| DATES | DURATION | SCRIPTURE |
|---|---|---|
| 853-845 | 8 YRS. | 2 KINGS 8:16-24; 2 CHRON. 21:1-20 |

1. HE MARRIED ATHALIAH, DAUGHTER OF AHAB AND JEZEBEL.
2. HE BEGAN HIS REIGN BY MURDERING HIS SIX BROTHERS.
3. HE RECEIVED A POST-HUMOUS MESSAGE FROM ELIJAH PREDICTING JUDGMENT UPON HIM BECAUSE OF HIS WICKED AND MURDEROUS REIGN.
4. HE WAS ATTACKED AND DEFEATED BY THE PHILISTINES AND ARABIANS.
5. HE DIED OF A HORRIBLE DISEASE AND WAS UNMOURNED AT THE FUNERAL.

## VI — AHAZIAH

| DATES | DURATION | SCRIPTURE |
|---|---|---|
| 841 | 1 YR. | 2 KINGS 8:24-9:29; 2 CHRON. 22:1-9 |

1. HE WAS THE SON OF JORAM AND ATHALIAH.
2. HE WAS KILLED BY JEHU (10th NORTHERN KING)

## VII — ATHALIAH

| DATES | DURATION | SCRIPTURE |
|---|---|---|
| 841-835 | 6 YRS | 2 KINGS 11:1-20; 2 CHRON. 22:1-23:21 |

1. AT THE DEATH OF AHAZIAH HER SON, SHE TOOK OVER THE JUDEAN THRONE, SLAUGHTERING ALL THE ROYAL SEED BUT ONE (JOASH) WHO WAS HIDDEN FROM HER.
2. AFTER A RULE OF 6 YEARS SHE HERSELF WAS EXECUTED

**JOASH**

| DATES | DURATION | SCRIPTURE |
|-------|----------|-----------|
| 835-795 | 40 YRS | 2 KINGS 11:1-12:21; 2 CHRON. 22:10-24:27 |

1. HE ALONE HAD SURVIVED ATHALIAH'S BLOOD PURGE.

2. FOR AWHILE HE LIVED FOR GOD BUT LATER BECAME A CRUEL TYRANT.

3. HE SANCTIONED THE STONING OF JUDAH'S OWN HIGH PRIEST, ZECHARIAH, WHO HAD FEARLESSLY REBUKED THE SIN AMONG THE PEOPLE.

4. HE WAS EXECUTED BY HIS OWN PALACE GUARD.

**AMAZIAH**

| DATES | DURATION | SCRIPTURE |
|-------|----------|-----------|
| 796-767 | 29 YRS. | 2 KINGS 14:1-20; 2 CHRON. 25:1-28 |

1. WAS A GOOD KING FOR AWHILE, EXECUTING THE KILLERS OF HIS FATHER JOASH.

2. WAS REBUKED BY A PROPHET FOR HIRING SOME MERCENARY ISRAELI SOLDIERS TO HELP HIM FIGHT AGAINST EDOM.

3. HE RELUCTANTLY DISMISSES THESE PAID SOLDIERS AND, WITH GOD'S HELP DEFEATS EDOM WITH HIS OWN SOLDIERS.

4. HE FOOLISHLY BRINGS BACK SOME OF THE EDOMITE GODS FOR WORSHIPPING PURPOSES.

5. THE RECKLESS KING THEN DECLARED WAR ON NORTHERN ISRAEL AND WAS SOUNDLY DEFEATED.

**UZZIAH**

| DATES | DURATION | SCRIPTURE |
|-------|----------|-----------|
| 792-740 | 52 YRS. | 2 KINGS 15:1-7; 2 CHRON. 26:1-23 |

1. WAS A MIGHTY WARRIOR AND BUILDER.

2. ATTEMPTED HOWEVER, TO INTRUDE INTO THE OFFICE OF THE PRIESTHOOD AND WAS PUNISHED FOR THIS BY LEPROSY.

| DATES | DURATION | SCRIPTURE |
|-------|----------|-----------|
| 750-736 | 16 YRS | 2 KINGS 15:32-38; 2 CHRON. 27:1-9 |

1. WAS A GOOD KING.

2. BUILT THE UPPER GATE OF THE TEMPLE AND ERECTED FORTRESSES AND TOWERS.

3. DEFEATED HIS ENEMIES AND RECEIVED HUGE ANNUAL TRIBUTE FROM THEM.

| DATES | DURATION | SCRIPTURE |
|-------|----------|-----------|
| 735-719 | 16 YRS. | 2 KINGS 16:1-20; 2 CHRON. 28:1-27 |

1. WAS PERHAPS THE SECOND WORST KING OF JUDAH.

2. SACRIFICED HIS OWN CHILDREN TO DEVIL GODS.

3. WAS FIRST PERSON TO HEAR ABOUT THE VIRGIN BIRTH. (SEE ISA. 7:1-25)

4. ORDERED THE CONSTRUCTION OF A PAGAN ASSYRIAN ALTAR AND PLACED IT IN THE TEMPLE TO APPEASE TIGLATH-PILESER.

| DATES | DURATION | SCRIPTURE |
|-------|----------|-----------|
| 716-687 | 29 YRS. | 2 KINGS 18:1-20;21; 2 CHRON. 29:1-32:33 |

1. WAS JUDAH'S SECOND BEST KING AND THE RICHEST OF ALL.

2. REPAIRED THE TEMPLE, ORGANIZED AN ORCHESTRAL GROUP AND APPOINTED A LEVITICAL SINGING CHOIR.

3. CARRIED OUT THE GREATEST PASSOVER CELEBRATION SINCE SOLOMON.

4. SAW THE DEATH ANGEL DEFEAT THE ASSYRIAN ENEMIES WHICH HAD SURROUNDED JERUSALEM.

5. WAS SUPERNATURALLY HEALED OF A TERMINAL DISEASE AND GIVEN AN ADDITIONAL 15 YEARS TO LIVE.

6. ADDED 15 PSALMS TO THE O.T. CANON.

7. FOOLISHLY SHOWED THE WEALTH OF JUDAH TO SOME NOSEY BABYLONIAN AMBASSADORS.

**XIV**

MANASSEH

| DATES | DURATION | SCRIPTURE |
|-------|----------|-----------|
| 697-642 | 55 YRS. | 2 KINGS 21:1-18; 2 CHRON. 33:1-20 |

1. HE RULED LONGER THAN ANY OTHER KING OF NORTH OR SOUTH.

2. HE WAS THE MOST WICKED KING OF ALL.

3. HE EXPERIENCED THE NEW BIRTH WHILE IN AN ENEMY PRISON.

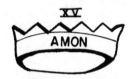

**XV**

AMON

| DATES | DURATION | SCRIPTURE |
|-------|----------|-----------|
| 643-641 | 2 YRS. | 2 KINGS 21:19-26; 2 CHRON. 33:21-25 |

1. WAS WICKED LIKE HIS FATHER, MANASSEH, BUT DID NOT REPENT AS DID HIS FATHER.

2. WAS EXECUTED BY HIS OWN HOUSEHOLD SERVANTS.

**XVI**

JOSIAH

| DATES | DURATION | SCRIPTURE |
|-------|----------|-----------|
| 641-610 | 31 YRS. | 2 KINGS 22:1-23:30; 2 CHRON. 34:1-35:27 |

1. WAS THE GODLIEST KING SINCE DAVID.

2. WAS JUDAH'S LAST SAVED KING.

3. THE BOOK OF MOSES WAS ACCIDENTALLY DISCOVERERED AMONG THE DEBRIS IN THE TEMPLE AT THE BEGINNING OF HIS REIGN.

4. HE USED THIS TO LEAD JUDAH IN A GREAT REVIVAL.

5. HE ALSO CONDUCTED A LARGER PASSOVER CELEBRATION THAN THAT OF HEZEKIAH HIS GREAT GRANDFATHER.

6. HE FULFILLED A 300-YEAR OLD PROPHECY. COMPARE I KINGS 13:1-2 WITH 2 KINGS 23:15.

7. HE WAS KILLED IN A BATTLE WITH THE EGYPTIANS.

XVII

JEHOAHAZ

| DATES | DURATION | SCRIPTURE |
|-------|----------|-----------|
| 609 | 3 MONTHS | 2 KINGS 23:31-33; 2 CHRON. 36:1-4 |

1. WAS THE MIDDLE SON OF JOSIAH.
2. WAS DEPOSED AFTER ONLY 90 DAYS BY THE PHARAOH WHO HAD KILLED HIS FATHER.
3. WAS CARRIED INTO EGYPTIAN CAPTIVITY WHERE HE EVENTUALLY DIED.

XVIII

JEHOIAKIM

| DATES | DURATION | SCRIPTURE |
|-------|----------|-----------|
| 609-598 | 11 YRS. | 2 KINGS 23:34-24:5; 2 CHRON. 36:5-7 |

1. WAS THE OLDEST BROTHER OF JEHOAHAZ.
2. WAS PUT ON THRONE BY THE EGYPTIAN PHARAOH.
3. WAS LATER MADE VASSAL BY NEBUCHADNEZZAR AFTER THE BABYLONIANS HAD DEFEATED THE EGYPTIANS.
4. WAS TOTALLY MATERIALISTIC AND SELF-CENTERED. HE CAN BE CONSIDERED AS JUDAH'S 3rd WORST KING.
5. HE MURDERED THE INNOCENT AND OFTEN PERSECUTED JEREMIAH.
6. HE BURNED A COPY OF A PART OF GOD'S WORD. SEE JER. 36:22-32.
7. HE EXPERIENCED THE FIRST OF THREE FEARFUL "VISITS" NEBUCHADNEZ-ZAR MADE TO THE CITY OF JERUSALEM.
8. DURING THIS VISIT (606 B.C.) DANIEL AND OTHER HEBREW YOUNG PEOPLE WERE CARRIED OFF INTO CAPTIVITY.
9. AT HIS DEATH HE RECEIVED THE BURIAL OF AN ASS, AS JEREMIAH HAD PREDICTED.

## XIX

**JEHOIACHIN**

| DATES | DURATION | SCRIPTURE |
|-------|----------|-----------|
| 598 | 3 MONTHS | 2 KINGS 24:6-16; 2 CHRON. 36:8-10 |

1. WAS THE SON OF JEHOIAKIM AND GRANDSON OF JOSIAH.
2. HE INCURRED UPON HIM A CURSE FROM GOD, STATING THAT HIS SONS WOULD NOT SIT UPON JUDAH'S THRONE.
3. BOTH EZEKIEL (19:5-9) AND JEREMIAH (22:24-26) PREDICTED HE WOULD BE CARRIED OFF INTO BABYLONIAN CAPTIVITY.
4. THIS HAPPENED DURING NEBUCHADNEZZAR'S SECOND "VISIT" (597) TO JERUSALEM. EZEKIEL WAS ALSO CARRIED AWAY AT THIS TIME.
5. HE EVENTUALLY DIES IN BABYLON.

## XX

**ZEDEKIAH**

| DATES | DURATION | SCRIPTURE |
|-------|----------|-----------|
| 597-586 | 11 YRS. | 2 KINGS 24:17-25:30; 2 CHRON. 36:11-21 |

1. WAS YOUNGEST SON OF JOSIAH AND UNCLE TO JEHOIACHIN.
2. JEREMIAH WAS PERSECUTED DURING HIS REIGN.
3. REBELLED AGAINST BABYLON ALONG WITH EGYPT.
4. WAS CAPTURED, BLINDED, AND CARRIED OFF INTO BABYLONIAN CAPTIVITY BY NEBUCHADNEZZAR.
5. JERUSALEM IS BURNED TO THE GROUND AND THE TEMPLE DESTROYED AT THIS TIME.

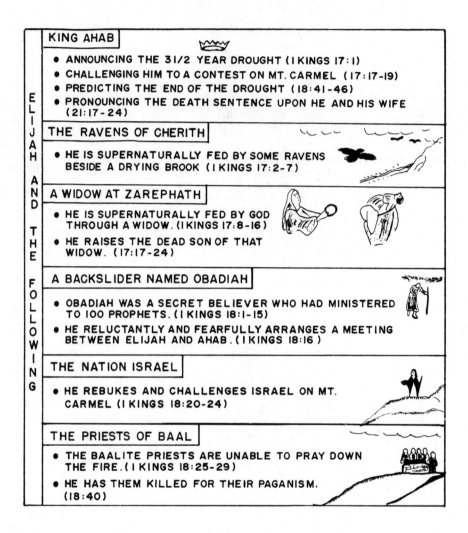

**KING AHAB**

- ANNOUNCING THE 3 1/2 YEAR DROUGHT (I KINGS 17:1)
- CHALLENGING HIM TO A CONTEST ON MT. CARMEL (17:17-19)
- PREDICTING THE END OF THE DROUGHT (18:41-46)
- PRONOUNCING THE DEATH SENTENCE UPON HE AND HIS WIFE (21:17-24)

**THE RAVENS OF CHERITH**

- HE IS SUPERNATURALLY FED BY SOME RAVENS BESIDE A DRYING BROOK (I KINGS 17:2-7)

**A WIDOW AT ZAREPHATH**

- HE IS SUPERNATURALLY FED BY GOD THROUGH A WIDOW. (I KINGS 17:8-16)
- HE RAISES THE DEAD SON OF THAT WIDOW. (17:17-24)

**A BACKSLIDER NAMED OBADIAH**

- OBADIAH WAS A SECRET BELIEVER WHO HAD MINISTERED TO 100 PROPHETS. (I KINGS 18:1-15)
- HE RELUCTANTLY AND FEARFULLY ARRANGES A MEETING BETWEEN ELIJAH AND AHAB. (I KINGS 18:16)

**THE NATION ISRAEL**

- HE REBUKES AND CHALLENGES ISRAEL ON MT. CARMEL (I KINGS 18:20-24)

**THE PRIESTS OF BAAL**

- THE BAALITE PRIESTS ARE UNABLE TO PRAY DOWN THE FIRE. (I KINGS 18:25-29)
- HE HAS THEM KILLED FOR THEIR PAGANISM. (18:40)

ELIJAH AND THE FOLLOWING

# ELIJAH THE PROPHET

## THE LORD GOD

- HE FLEES ISRAEL TO ESCAPE JEZEBEL'S REVENGE. ( I KINGS 19:1-3)
- HE IS MINISTERED TO BY AN ANGEL. (19:4-7)
- HE HEARS GOD'S STILL SMALL VOICE IN A CAVE. (19:8-18)

## ELISHA THE PROPHET

- HE CALLS ELISHA TO SPECIAL SERVICE. (I KINGS 19:19-21)
- HE PREPARE ELISHA FOR SPECIAL SERVICE. ( 2 KINGS 2:1-10)

## NORTHERN KING AHAZIAH

- HE PREDICTS WICKED AHAZIAH WOULD DIE FROM A FALL HE HAD SUSTAINED (2 KINGS 1:1-18)
- HE PRAYS DOWN FIRE TO DESTROY TWO COMPANIES OF SOLDIERS SENT TO ARREST HIM (1:9-12)
- HE SPARES THE 3rd COMPANY, LED BY A CAPTAIN WHO BEGGED FOR MERCY (1:13-16)

## A CHARIOT OF FIRE

- HE PARTS THE RIVER JORDAN AND STANDS ON THE EASTERN BANK (2 KINGS 2:1-8)
- HE RECEIVES A LAST REQUEST FROM ELISHA (2:9-10)
- HE IS CARRIED INTO HEAVEN WITHOUT DYING (2:11)

ELIJAH AND THE FOLLOWING

# ELISHA
## AND
## EIGHTEEN EXCITING EVENTS

### ONE
PARTING THE WATERS AT JORDAN-2 KINGS 2:14

### TWO
PURIFYING THE WATERS AT JERICHO-2 KINGS 2:19-22

### THREE
JUDGING SOME HOODLUMS AT BETHEL 2 KINGS 2: 23,24

### FOUR
CAUSING SOME EMPTY DITCHES TO FILL WITH WATER – 2 KINGS 3:16-27

### FIVE
CREATING OIL IN EMPTY VESSELS-2 KINGS 4:1-7

### SIX
RAISING A DEAD BOY AT SHUNAM - 2 KINGS 4:18-21; 32-37

### SEVEN
PURIFYING A POISONOUS STEW AT GILGAL – 2 KINGS 4:38-41

### EIGHT
FEEDING 100 MEN BY SUPERNATURALLY INCREASING 20 LOAVES OF BREAD AND A SACK OF CORN 4:42-44

### NINE
HEALING OF NAAMAN FROM LEPROSY 2KINGS 5:1-14

## TEN

PREDICTING THE JUDGMENT OF LEPROSY UPON GEHAZI - 2 KINGS 5:15-27

## ELEVEN

RECOVERING A LOST AXHEAD FROM THE JORDAN 2 KINGS 6:1-7

## TWELVE

REVEALING THE SECRET WAR PLANS OF SYRIA TO ISRAEL - 2 KINGS 6:8-12

## THIRTEEN

PRAYING THAT HIS SERVANT WOULD SEE AN INVISIBLE ANGELIC ARMY - 2 KINGS 6:13-17

## FOURTEEN

BLINDING THE ENTIRE SYRIAN ARMY 2KINGS 6:18-23

## FIFTEEN

PROMISING DELIVERANCE TO THE STARVING CITIZENS OF SAMARIA - 2 KINGS 6:24-7:20

## SIXTEEN

PREDICTING THE DEATH OF BENHADAD, KING OF SYRIA AND THE SUBSEQUENT REIGN OF HAZAEL OVER SYRIA - 2 KINGS 8:7-15

## SEVENTEEN

PREDICTING THREE VICTORIES BY ISRAEL OVER SYRIA - 2 KINGS 13:14-19

## EIGHTEEN

RAISING A DEAD MAN YEARS AFTER ELISHA HIMSELF HAD DIED - 2KINGS 13:20,21

# THE WRITING PROPHETS OF THE CHAOTIC KINGDOM STAGE

| AUTHOR | LENGTH OF MINISTRY | DATES | DESTINATION |
|---|---|---|---|
| 1. OBADIAH | 10 | 850 - 840 | EDOM |
| 2. JONAH | 35 | 785 - 750 | NINEVEH |
| 3. NAHUM | 30 | 650 - 620 | NINEVEH |
| 4. AMOS | 7 | 760 - 753 | NORTH (ISRAEL) |
| 5. HOSEA | 60 | 760 - 700 | NORTH |
| 6. JOEL | 7 | 841 - 834 | SOUTH (JUDAH) |
| 7. ISAIAH | 58 | 739 - 681 | SOUTH |
| 8. MICAH | 35 | 735 - 700 | SOUTH |
| 9. ZEPHANIAH | 20 | 640 - 620 | SOUTH |
| 10. HABAKKUK | 3 | 609 - 606 | SOUTH |
| 11. JEREMIAH | 32 | 627 - 575 | SOUTH |
| 12. LAMENTATIONS | — | 586 | SOUTH |

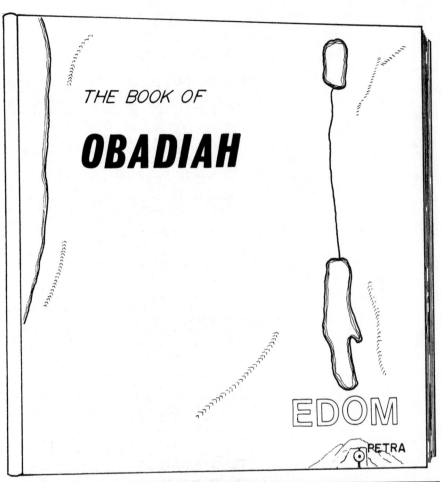

THE BOOK OF

# OBADIAH

EDOM

PETRA

| THEME OF BOOK | THE DESTRUCTION OF THE NATION EDOM |
|---|---|
| FOUNDER OF NATION | ESAU, BROTHER OF JACOB |
| REASONS FOR DESTRUCTION | • BECAUSE OF THEIR THANKLESS HEART (1:3-9)<br>• BECAUSE OF THEIR TREACHEROUS HAND (1:10-14) |
| FUTURE OF NATION | • LAND TO BE OCCUPIED BY THE NATION ISRAEL (1:17-20)<br>• LAND TO BE BLESSED BY THE GOD OF ISRAEL (1:21) |

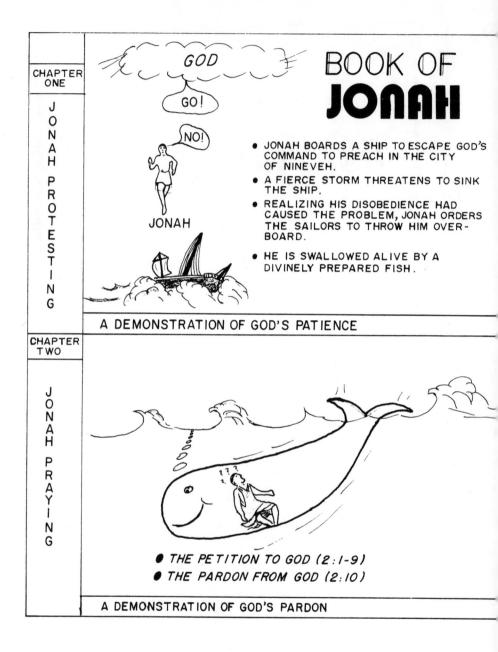

BOOK OF
# JONAH

**CHAPTER ONE**

J O N A H   P R O T E S T I N G

- JONAH BOARDS A SHIP TO ESCAPE GOD'S COMMAND TO PREACH IN THE CITY OF NINEVEH.
- A FIERCE STORM THREATENS TO SINK THE SHIP.
- REALIZING HIS DISOBEDIENCE HAD CAUSED THE PROBLEM, JONAH ORDERS THE SAILORS TO THROW HIM OVER-BOARD.
- HE IS SWALLOWED ALIVE BY A DIVINELY PREPARED FISH.

A DEMONSTRATION OF GOD'S PATIENCE

**CHAPTER TWO**

J O N A H   P R A Y I N G

- *THE PETITION TO GOD (2:1-9)*
- *THE PARDON FROM GOD (2:10)*

A DEMONSTRATION OF GOD'S PARDON

| CHAPTER THREE | • THE WARNING FROM THE PROPHET (3:1-4) |
|---|---|

| CHAPTER THREE | • THE WARNING FROM THE PROPHET (3:1-4) |  |
|---|---|---|
| J O N A H  P R E A C H I N G | • THE WARNING FROM THE PROPHET (3:1-4) | |
| | REPENT! | |
| | • THE MOURNING BY THE PEOPLE (3:4-9) | |
| | WE DO! | |
| | • THE TRANSFORMING BY THE LORD (3:10) | |
| | I FORGIVE! | |
| | A DEMONSTRATION OF GOD'S POWER | |
| CHAPTER FOUR | LAMENTING OVER A CITY! | LEARNING UNDER A GOURD! |
| J O N A H  P O U T I N G | • THE CARNAL JONAH WATCHES, STILL HOPING THE REVIVAL WOULD BE SHORT-LIVED SO THAT GOD COULD DESTROY NINEVEH. | • GOD ATTEMPTS TO CORRECT JONAH BY CREATING A GOURD, AND THEN ALLOWING THE SUN TO KILL IT. |
| | | |
| | A DEMONSTRATION OF GOD'S PITY | |

# BOOK OF NAHUM
## THE DESTRUCTION OF NINEVEH

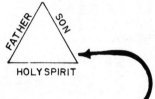

- SOURCE OF THE DESTRUCTION - GOD HIMSELF!
- REASON FOR THE DESTRUCTION - SIN!
- TOOL USED IN THE DESTRUCTION - BABYLON!

CRUELTY!

WICKEDNESS!

EVIL!

---

### I

**THE PATIENCE OF GOD**

(1:8)

- GOD HAD ONCE STAYED HIS HAND OF JUDGMENT UPON NINEVEH THROUGH JONAH'S MINISTRY. BUT NOW HIS PATIENCE WAS EXHAUSTED.

### II

**THE PRIDE OF THE ASSYRIAN KING**

(1:9-14)

### III

**THE PROMISE TO JUDAH**

(1:15)

- JUDAH NEED NO LONGER FEAR THIS CRUEL NATION.

### IV

**THE PUNISHMENT OF NINEVEH**

(2-3)

- THE CERTAINTY OF IT (3:11:19)
- THE DESCRIPTION OF IT (2:3-9)

# 𝕬𝕸𝕺𝕾

## PART ONE

| EIGHT NATIONS DENOUNCED (1-6) | | |
|---|---|---|
| NATION | CRIME | PUNISHMENT |
| SYRIA (1:1-5) | HAD OFTEN HARASSED ISRAEL | • THE CAPITAL AT DAMASCUS TO BE BURNED<br>• THEIR STRONGHOLDS TO BE BROKEN<br>• THEIR CITIZENS TO BE ENSLAVED |
| PHILISTIA (1:6-8) | HAD SOLD ISRAELITES INTO SLAVERY TO EDOM | • THE BURNING OF THEIR FOUR MAIN CITIES: GAZA, ASHDOD, ASHKELON, EKRON |
| PHOENICIA (1:9-10) | HAD BROKEN THEIR PEACE COVENANT WITH ISRAEL | • THE BURNING DOWN OF THE FORTS AND PALACES IN TYRE, THEIR CHIEF CITY. |
| EDOM (1:11-12) | HAD MURDERED MANY JEWS | • THE DESTRUCTION OF THEIR CITIES |
| AMMON (1:13-15) | HAD MURDERED JEWISH WOMEN | • THEIR CITIES TO BE BURNED<br>• THEIR CITIZENS TO BE ENSLAVED |
| MOAB (2:1-3) | HAD DESECRATED THE TOMBS OF THE DEAD | • THEY WOULD BE DEFEATED IN BATTLE |
| JUDAH (2:4-5) | • HAD REJECTED THE WORD OF GOD<br>• HAD DISOBEYED THE GOD OF THE WORD | • THEIR TEMPLE IN JERUSALEM TO BE DESTROYED |
| ISRAEL (2:6-16) | • HAD ACCEPTED BRIBES<br>• HAD ENSLAVED THE POOR<br>• HAD COMMITTED ADULTERY<br>• HAD STOLEN<br>• WERE TOTALLY UNTHANKFUL<br>• HAD CAUSED THE INNOCENT TO SIN. | • THEIR PUNISHMENT WOULD MAKE THEM GROAN AS A LOADED-DOWN WAGON<br>• THEIR ARMIES WOULD STUMBLE IN BATTLE |
| *ADDITIONAL INDICTMENTS UPON THE WHOLE HOUSE OF ISRAEL – BOTH SOUTHERN AND NORTHERN KINGDOMS (3-6)* | | |

# AMOS
## PART TWO

- THE LOCUST PLAGUE
     ( 7:1-3 )

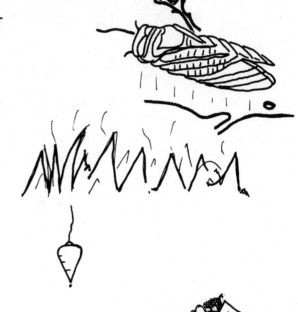

- THE GREAT FIRE
     ( 7:4-6 )

- THE PLUMB LINE
     ( 7:7-16 )

- THE BASKET OF SUMMER FRUIT
     ( 8:1-4 )

- THE LORD AT THE ALTAR
     ( 9:1-15 )

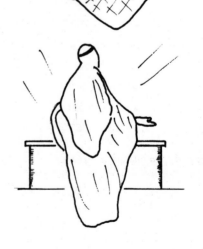

# A GRIEVING HUSBAND AND HIS GRIEVOUS WIFE

## HOSEA AND GOMER (1-3)

### HIS WIFE-ILL FAMED

- GOMER WAS A HARLOT BEFORE MARRIAGE AND AN ADULTERESS AFTER MARRIAGE.

- HOSEA ATTEMPTS TO SAVE HIS MARRIAGE BY:
  1. Barring Gomer from the Markets of the World.
  2. Buying her out of the Markets of the World.
  3. Asking his own son to reason with his Mother.

### HIS CHILDREN- ILL NAMED

| NAME | MEANING |
|------|---------|
| JEZREEL | "To be scattered" This Predicted Two Things: <br> 1. Scattering of JEHU'S Seed. <br> 2. Scattering of Northern Kingdom |
| LO-RUHA-MAH | "NO MORE MERCY" |
| LO-AMMI | "NOT MY PEOPLE" |

## EPHRAIM AND GOD (4-14)

- EPHRAIM DENOUNCED
  1. BECAUSE OF HER IGNORANCE (4:6)
  2. BECAUSE OF HER IDOLATRY (4:12,13,17)
  3. BECAUSE OF HER IMMORALITY (5:3)

- EPHRAIM DESIRED (6:4)
  IN SPITE OF ALL THIS, GOD STILL LOVED HER!

- EPHRAIM DESCRIBED
  1. A BACKSLIDING HEIFER (4:16)
  2. A BAKER'S HOT OVEN (7:4)
  3. A HALF-BAKED CAKE (7:8)
  4. A SILLY DOVE (7:11)
  5. A CROOKED BOW (7:16)
  6. A BROKEN POT (8:8)
  7. A WANDERING AND LONELY WILD ANIMAL (8:9)
  8. A DRIED UP ROOT (9:16)
  9. AN EMPTY VINE (10:1)

- EPHRAIM DISCIPLINED (3:4)
  TO BE MANY DAYS WITHOUT:
  1. A KING          4. AN IMAGE
  2. A PRINCE        5. AN EPHOD
  3. A SACRIFICE     6. TERAPHIM

- EPHRAIM DELIVERED
  1. 2:19,23     4. 11:1,4,8,9
  2. 3:5         5. 13:10,14
  3. 6:1-3       6. 14:4-7

BOOK OF HOSEA

HOSEA

## CONTEMPORARY EVENTS (1)

### A REVIEW OF ISRAEL'S CURRENT INSECT INVASION

- NATURE: A TERRIBLE LOCUST PLAGUE HAD SETTLED DOWN UPON THE LAND (1:4,12)

- REASON: BECAUSE OF ISRAEL'S SIN (1:5)

- SUGGESTED CURE: CALL FOR A SPECIAL MEETING, PRAY, AND REPENT! (1:14)

## COMING EVENTS (2-3)

### A PREVIEW OF ISRAEL'S COMING ENEMY INVASION.

- IDENTITY: PROBABLY TWO-FOLD:
  1. THE RUSSIAN INVASION DURING THE MIDDLE OF THE TRIBULATION, LED BY GOG (EZEK. 38-39)
  2. THE FINAL INVASION AT THE END OF THE TRIBULATION, LED BY ANTICHRIST (REV.16:13-16; 19:11-21)

- LOCATION: VALLEY OF JEHOSHAPHAT (3:2, 9-14)

- PURPOSE:
  1. THE PURPOSE OF SATAN - TO DESTROY ISRAEL AND HER GOD. (PSALM 2)
  2. THE PURPOSE OF GOD - TO DESTROY SATAN AND HIS ALLIES (REV.16:16)

- RESULTS:
  1. THE SALVATION OF ISRAEL (3:15-21)
  2. THE SANCTIFICATION OF ISRAEL (2:21-32)

THE PROPHET USES AN EVENT CONTEMPORARY IN HIS DAY TO

*DESCRIBE COMING EVENTS*

# THE BOOK OF JOEL

162

# GENERAL OUTLINE OF ISAIAH

## 1-35

*ISRAEL – GOD'S FAITHLESS SERVANT*

| | |
|---|---|
| 1,3,5 | HER SINS LISTED |
| 2,4,9,11,12,22,25-35 | HER FUTURE PREDICTED |
| 6 | HER HOLY GOD |
| 7 | HER VIRGIN BORN MESSIAH |
| 13-25 | HER ENEMIES JUDGED |

## 36-39

*HEZEKIAH – GOD'S FRIGHTENED SERVANT*

| | |
|---|---|
| 36-37 | HEZEKIAH AND THE KING OF ASSYRIA |
| 38 | HEZEKIAH AND THE KING OF HEAVEN |
| 39 | HEZEKIAH AND THE KING OF BABYLON |

## 40-66

*CHRIST – GOD'S FAITHFUL SERVANT*

| | | |
|---|---|---|
| 40 - 48 | THE DELIVERANCE | THE COMFORT OF JEHOVAH<br>● GOD AND THE IDOLS (40-46)<br>● GOD AND THE NATIONS (47-48) |
| 49-57 | THE DELIVERER | THE SALVATION OF JEHOVAH |
| 58-66 | THE DELIVERED | THE GLORY OF JEHOVAH |

ISAIAH

163

# A SUMMARY OF ISAIAH'S PROPHECIES

| | |
|---|---|
| THOSE FULFILLED DURING ISAIAH'S LIFETIME | A. JUDAH WOULD BE SAVED FROM THE THREATENED SYRIAN AND ISRAELITE INVASION (7:4,16) |
| | B. SYRIA AND ISRAEL LATER TO BE DESTROYED BY ASSYRIA (8:4;17:1-14;28:1) |
| | C. ASSYRIA WOULD INVADE JUDAH (8:7-8) |
| | D. JERUSALEM WOULD BE SAVED DURING THIS INVASION (37:33-35) |
| | E. MOAB WOULD BE JUDGED BY THE ASSYRIANS WITHIN THREE YEARS (15-16) |
| | F. EGYPT AND ETHIOPIA WOULD BE CONQUERED BY THE ASSYRIANS (18,19,20) |
| | G. ARABIA WOULD BE DESTROYED (21:13-17) |
| | H. TYRE TO BE DESTROYED (23:1-12) |
| | I. HEZEKIAH'S LIFE WOULD BE EXTENDED BY 15 YEARS (38:5) |
| | J. ASSYRIA TO BE JUDGED BY GOD (10:5-34; 14:24; 30:27-33; 37:36) |
| THOSE FULFILLED AFTER ISAIAH'S DEATH | A. THE BABYLONIAN CAPTIVITY (3:1-8; 5:26-30; 22:1-14; 39:5-7) |
| | B. BABYLON TO BE OVERTHROWN BY CYRUS (13:17; 21:2; 48:14; 46:11; 13:17-22; 14:1-23) |
| | C. BABYLON TO SUFFER PERPETUAL DESOLATION (13:20-22; 47:1-15) |
| | D. THE CONQUESTS OF A PERSIAN NAMED CYRUS (44:28; 45:1,4; 41:2-3) |
| | E. THE RETURN TO JERUSALEM DECREE OF CYRUS (44:38; 45:13) |
| | F. THE JOY OF THE RETURNING REMNANT (48:20; ALSO COMPARE THIS WITH PSA.126) |
| | G. THE RESTORATION OF TYRE (23:13-18) |
| | H. THE PERPETUAL DESOLATION OF EDOM (34:5-17) |
| | I. THE BIRTH, EARTHLY LIFE, SUFFERINGS, DEATH, RESURRECTION, ASCENSION, AND EXALTATION OF JESUS CHRIST. |
| | J. THE MINISTRY OF JOHN THE BAPTIST (ISA.40:3-5) |
| THOSE YET TO BE FULFILLED | A. THE TRIBULATION |
| | B. THE BATTLE OF ARMAGEDDON |
| | C. THE MILLENNIUM |

164

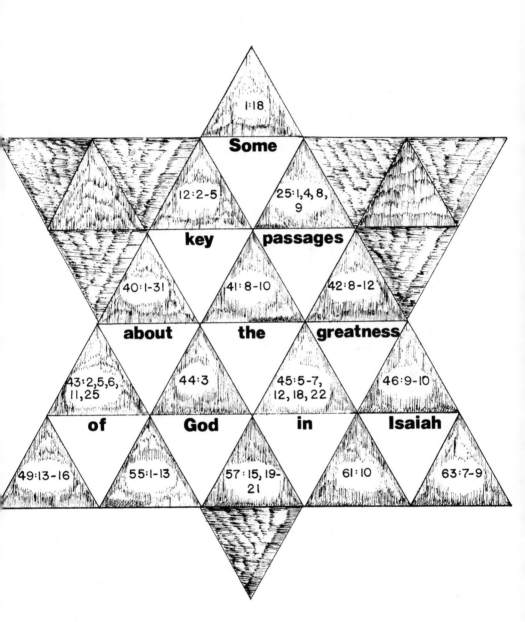

Some key passages about the greatness of God in Isaiah

1:18
12:2-5
25:1,4,8,9
40:1-31
41:8-10
42:8-12
43:2,5,6,11,25
44:3
45:5-7,12,18,22
46:9-10
49:13-16
55:1-13
57:15,19-21
61:10
63:7-9

# Christ in Isaiah

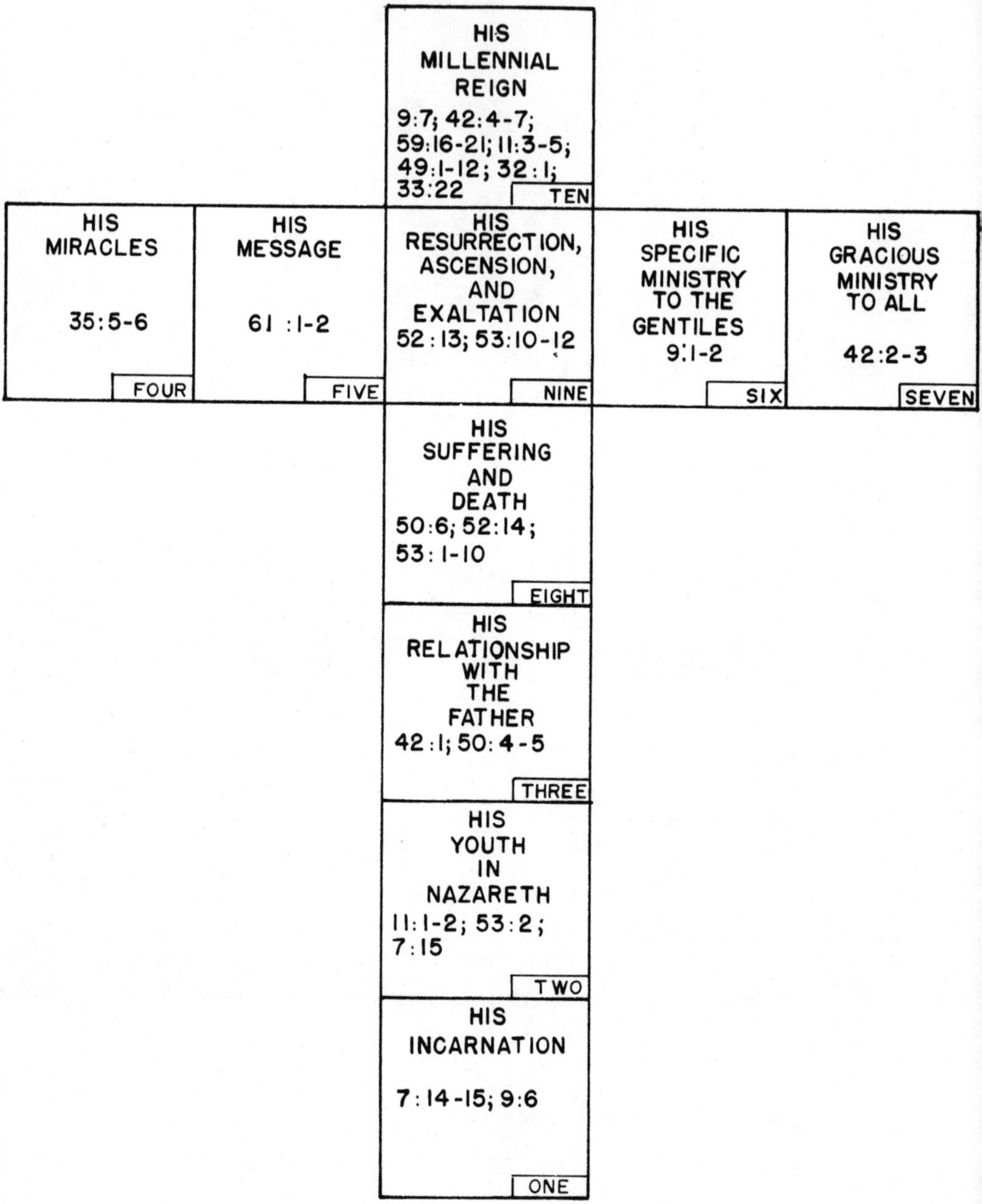

**HIS MILLENNIAL REIGN**

9:7; 42:4-7; 59:16-21; 11:3-5; 49:1-12; 32:1; 33:22

TEN

| HIS MIRACLES | HIS MESSAGE | HIS RESURRECTION, ASCENSION, AND EXALTATION | HIS SPECIFIC MINISTRY TO THE GENTILES | HIS GRACIOUS MINISTRY TO ALL |
|---|---|---|---|---|
| 35:5-6 | 61:1-2 | 52:13; 53:10-12 | 9:1-2 | 42:2-3 |
| FOUR | FIVE | NINE | SIX | SEVEN |

**HIS SUFFERING AND DEATH**

50:6; 52:14; 53:1-10

EIGHT

**HIS RELATIONSHIP WITH THE FATHER**

42:1; 50:4-5

THREE

**HIS YOUTH IN NAZARETH**

11:1-2; 53:2; 7:15

TWO

**HIS INCARNATION**

7:14-15; 9:6

ONE

# THE TRIBULATION IN ISAIAH

## MAIN PASSAGES

- 2:10-22
- 13:6-13
- 24:1-23
- 26:20-21
- 34:1-10
- 42:13-14
- 51:6
- 63:1-6
- 66:15-16

## MAIN ACTION

### EARTH

- TO BE SHAKEN
- TO BE MOVED OUT OF ITS PLACE
- TO BE MADE WASTE AND TURNED UPSIDE DOWN
- TO BE BURNED WITH FIRE
- TO BE BROKEN AND DISSOLVED
- TO REEL TO AND FRO LIKE A DRUNKARD
- TO BE UNABLE TO COVER ITS DEAD

### HEAVENS

- STARS, SUN AND MOON TO BE DARKENED
- HOSTS OF HEAVEN TO BE DISSOLVED AND ROLLED UP LIKE A SCROLL
- STARS TO FALL AS FIGS FROM A TREE WHEN SHAKEN

### SINFUL MANKIND

- TO HIDE IN CAVES AND HOLES OF THE EARTH
- TO FAINT WITH FEAR AND HEARTS TO MELT
- TO SUFFER THE PAIN OF CHILDBIRTH
- TO EXPERIENCE NO JOY WHATSOEVER
- TO COVER THE MOUNTAINS WITH THEIR DEAD
- TO OVERPOWER THE VALLEYS WITH THEIR STENCH.
- TO BE TRAMPED BY GOD LIKE OVER-RIPE GRAPES

OF GENTILE NATIONS

2:2-4; 11:10; 19:18-25; 52:10; 56:6-8

OF ISRAEL AND JERUSALEM

4:2-6; 11:12; 14:3; 30:19; 32:18; 44:23; 49:10-13; 51:3,11; 52:1,6-9; 59:20-21; 60:1-3,11-13, 19-22; 62:1-4; 65:18-24 66:10,12

OF THE AFFLICTED

29:18; 35:3-6; 42:16

OF ALL NATURE

11:6-9; 14:7-8; 30:23-26; 35:1,2,7-10; 40:4-5; 65:25

FOUR-FOLD SALVATION

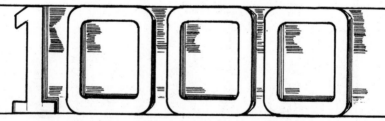

THE MILLENNIUM IN ISAIAH

# THE BOOK OF MICAH

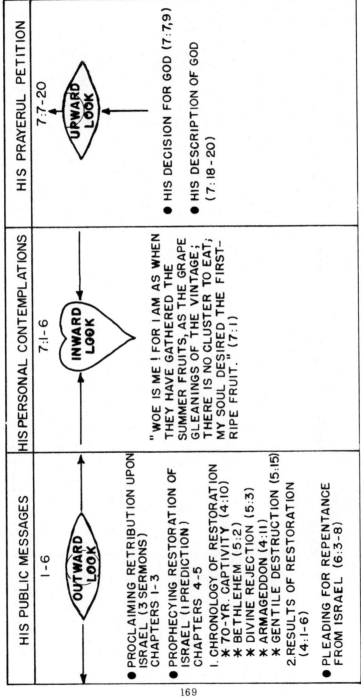

| HIS PUBLIC MESSAGES | HIS PERSONAL CONTEMPLATIONS | HIS PRAYERUL PETITION |
|---|---|---|
| 1-6 | 7:1-6 | 7:7-20 |
| OUTWARD LOOK | INWARD LOOK | UPWARD LOOK |

**HIS PUBLIC MESSAGES**

- PROCLAIMING RETRIBUTION UPON ISRAEL (3 SERMONS) CHAPTERS 1-3
- PROPHECYING RESTORATION OF ISRAEL (1 PREDICTION) CHAPTERS 4-5
  1. CHRONOLOGY OF RESTORATION
     * 70-YR. CAPTIVITY (4:10)
     * BETHLEHEM (5:2)
     * DIVINE REJECTION (5:3)
     * ARMAGEDDON (4:11)
     * GENTILE DESTRUCTION (5:15)
  2. RESULTS OF RESTORATION (4:1-6)
- PLEADING FOR REPENTANCE FROM ISRAEL (6:3-8)

**HIS PERSONAL CONTEMPLATIONS**

"WOE IS ME! FOR I AM AS WHEN THEY HAVE GATHERED THE SUMMER FRUITS, AS THE GRAPE GLEANINGS OF THE VINTAGE; THERE IS NO CLUSTER TO EAT; MY SOUL DESIRED THE FIRST-RIPE FRUIT." (7:1)

**HIS PRAYERUL PETITION**

- HIS DECISION FOR GOD (7:7,9)
- HIS DESCRIPTION OF GOD (7:18-20)

# THE BOOK OF ZEPHANIAH

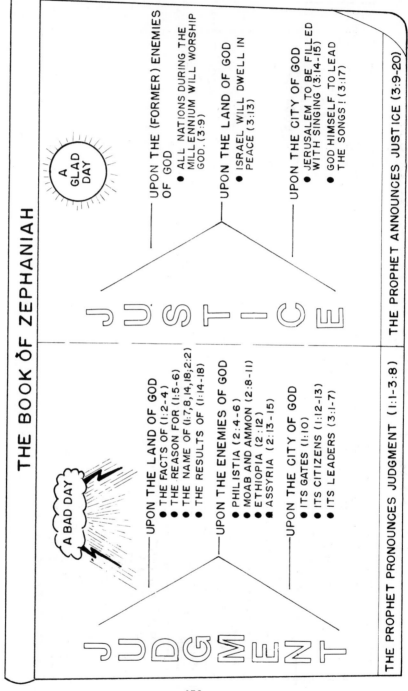

A BAD DAY

**J U D G M E N T**

UPON THE LAND OF GOD
- THE FACTS OF (1:2-4)
- THE REASON FOR (1:5-6)
- THE NAME OF (1:7,8,14,18;2:2)
- THE RESULTS OF (1:14-18)

UPON ITS ENEMIES OF GOD
- PHILISTIA (2:4-6)
- MOAB AND AMMON (2:8-11)
- ETHIOPIA (2:12)
- ASSYRIA (2:13-15)

UPON THE CITY OF GOD
- ITS GATES (1:10)
- ITS CITIZENS (1:12-13)
- ITS LEADERS (3:1-7)

A GLAD DAY

**J U S T I C E**

UPON THE (FORMER) ENEMIES OF GOD
- ALL NATIONS DURING THE MILLENNIUM WILL WORSHIP GOD. (3:9)

UPON THE LAND OF GOD
- ISRAEL WILL DWELL IN PEACE (3:13)

UPON THE CITY OF GOD
- JERUSALEM TO BE FILLED WITH SINGING (3:14-15)
- GOD HIMSELF TO LEAD THE SONGS! (3:17)

| THE PROPHET PRONOUNCES JUDGMENT (1:1-3:8) | THE PROPHET ANNOUNCES JUSTICE (3:9-20) |
| --- | --- |

170

# THE BOOK OF HABAKKUK

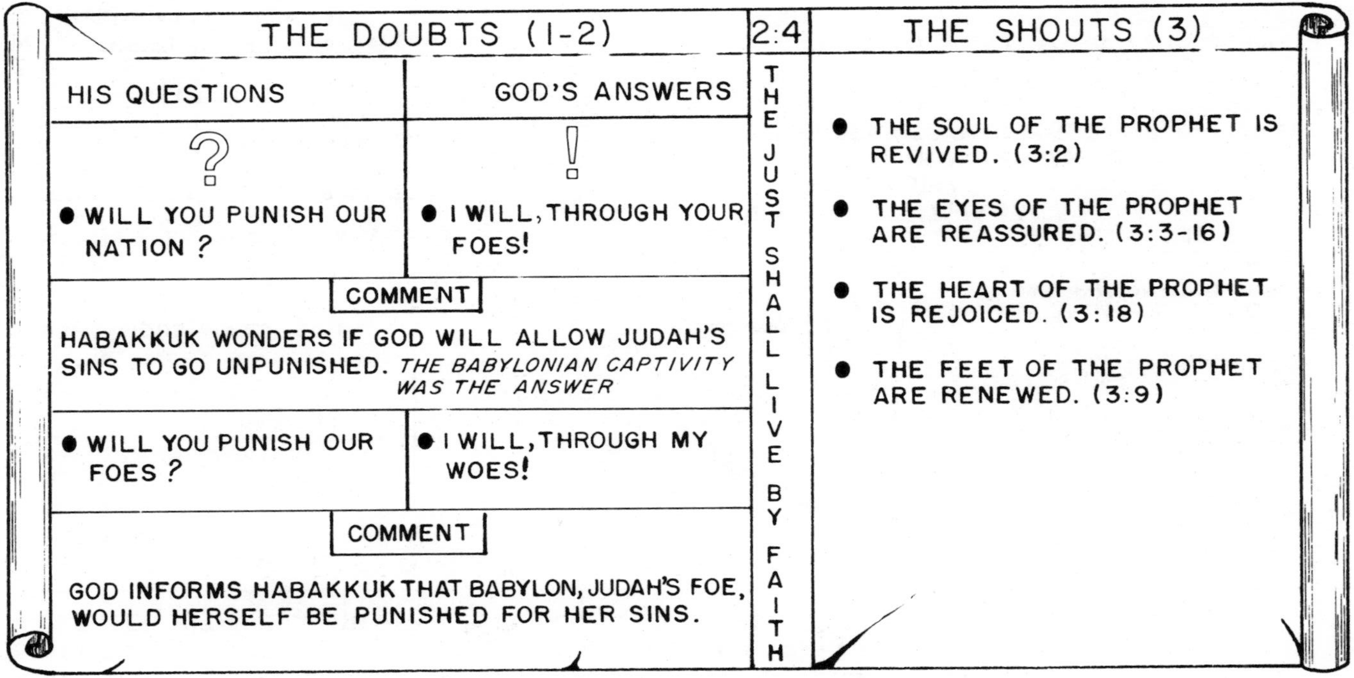

## THE DOUBTS (1-2)

| HIS QUESTIONS | GOD'S ANSWERS |
|---|---|
| ? | ! |
| ● WILL YOU PUNISH OUR NATION ? | ● I WILL, THROUGH YOUR FOES! |

**COMMENT**

HABAKKUK WONDERS IF GOD WILL ALLOW JUDAH'S SINS TO GO UNPUNISHED. *THE BABYLONIAN CAPTIVITY WAS THE ANSWER*

| | |
|---|---|
| ● WILL YOU PUNISH OUR FOES ? | ● I WILL, THROUGH MY WOES! |

**COMMENT**

GOD INFORMS HABAKKUK THAT BABYLON, JUDAH'S FOE, WOULD HERSELF BE PUNISHED FOR HER SINS.

**2:4** THE JUST SHALL LIVE BY FAITH

## THE SHOUTS (3)

- THE SOUL OF THE PROPHET IS REVIVED. (3:2)
- THE EYES OF THE PROPHET ARE REASSURED. (3:3-16)
- THE HEART OF THE PROPHET IS REJOICED. (3:18)
- THE FEET OF THE PROPHET ARE RENEWED. (3:9)

1. WAS THE SON OF A PRIEST (1:1)
2. WAS COMMANDED TO REMAIN UNMARRIED (16:2)
3. PROTESTED HIS CALL BY GOD AT FIRST, PLEADING YOUTH AS AN EXCUSE (1:6)
4. WAS ASSURED THAT GOD HAD ALREADY CHOSEN HIM EVEN PRIOR TO BIRTH (1:5)
5. ATTEMPTED TO FIND ONE HONEST MAN IN JERUSALEM (5:1-5)
6. PLEADED WITH JUDAH TO RETURN TO GOD (3:12-14; 26:1-7)

8. LISTS JUDAH'S MANY SINS
   - THEIR WORSHIP OF THE QUEEN OF HEAVEN (7:18, 44:17)
   - THEIR SACRIFICE OF THEIR OWN CHILDREN TO DEVIL GODS (8:31; 9:15)
   - THEIR MURDER OF JUDAH'S OWN PROPHETS (2:30)

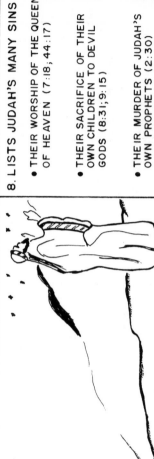

7. FEARLESSLY DENOUNCES JUDAH'S SIN AND IS PERSECUTED BY:
   - HIS FAMILY (12:6)
   - HOME TOWN PEOPLE (11:21)
   - RELIGIOUS WORLD (20:1-3; 26:7-9; 37:11-16)

9. WARNS THEM ABOUT COMING BABYLONIAN CAPTIVITY
   - JERUSALEM TO BE SURROUNDED (4:17; 6:3-5)
   - OWN TREES TO BE USED AGAINST HER (6:6)
   - TEMPLE TO BE DESTROYED (7:14)
   - CORPSES TO FEED ANIMALS (7:32; 9:22; 12:8-9)
   - CAPTIVITY FOR 70 YRS. (7:15; 25:11; 29:10)

10. WEEPS OVER THIS CAPTIVITY (4:19-21; 8:18,21; 9:1-2,10; 13:17; 14:17)
11. HAS HIS ORIGINAL MANUSCRIPT BURNED BY KING JEHOIAKIM (36:21-23)
12. THREATENS TO RESIGN (20:7-9, 14-18)
13. ORDERED TO BUY A FIELD WHILE IN PRISON TO PROVE A POINT (32:6-15)

14. IS FREED BY NEBUCHADNEZZAR (40:1-6; 39:14)
15. HELPS NEWLY APPOINTED GOVERNOR GEDALIAH (40:6)
16. ADVISES JOHANAN WHEN GEDALIAH IS KILLED (42:1-5)

17. IS CARRIED BY FORCE TO EGYPT BY JOHANAN (43:1-7)
18. CONTINUES TO PREACH OUT AGAINST SIN (43-44)
19. PROBABLY DIES IN EGYPT.

Personal Life of JEREMIAH

## "I ORDAINED THEE A PROPHET UNTO THE NATIONS"

| RULERS HE MINISTERED UNDER | PEOPLE HE MINISTERED TO | NATIONS HE PROPHECIED AGAINST | |
|---|---|---|---|
| **JOSIAH** JUDAH'S LAST SAVED KING | **I** • TO THE MAJORITY IN JUDAH ABOUT THE COMING CAPTIVITY - A WARNING | EGYPT 46:1-27 | • TO BE DEFEATED BY NEBUCHADNEZZAR AT BATTLE OF CARCHEMISH |
| **JEHOIAKIM** UNGODLY BIBLE-BURNING KING | | PHILISTIA 47:1-6 | • TO BE OVERRUN AND DESTROYED BY THE EGYPTIANS |
| **JEHOIACHIN** A 90-DAY WONDER JUDGED BY GOD | **II** • TO THE MINORITY ALREADY CAPTIVE IN BABYLON- AN ENCOURAGMENT (SEE CHAPTER 29) | MOAB 48:1-47 | • TO BE CONQUERED BY BABYLON |
| **ZEDEKIAH** JUDAH'S FINAL KING | | AMMON 49:1-6 | • TO BE DESTROYED FOR SIN-ING AGAINST ISRAEL<br>• TO BE RE-ESTABLISHED DURING THE MILLENNIUM |
| **NEBUCHADNEZZAR** GREAT BABYLONIAN CONQUEROR | | EDOM 49:7-22 | • TO BECOME AS SODOM AND GOMORRAH |
| **GEDALIAH** BABYLONIAN APPOINTED GOVERNOR OF OCCU-PIED CITY OF JERUSALEM | | DAMASCUS 49:23-27 | • TO BE DESTROYED IN A SINGLE DAY |
| **JOHANAN** SUCCESSOR OF GEDALIAH WHO WAS ASSASSINATED. | | KEDAR AND HAZOR 49:28-35 | • TO BE DESTROYED BY NEBUCHADNEZZAR |
| | | ELAM 49:34-39 | • TO BE OVERRUN BY NEBUCHAD-NEZZAR<br>• TO BE RE-ESTABLISHED DURING THE MILLENNIUM |
| | | BABYLON 50:1-51:64 | • THESE PROPHECIES CONCERN TWO BABYLONS. SEE NEXT OUTLINE |

# THE TWO BABYLONS OF JEREMIAH 50-51

| HISTORICAL BABYLON | FUTURE BABYLON |
|---|---|
| WAS CAPTURED BY DARIUS THE PERSIAN IN 539 B.C. | WILL BE DESTROYED BY GOD THE FATHER DURING THE TRIBULATION. SEE REV. 18:18 |

- AFTER THE FINAL DESTRUCTION OF BABYLON (REV. 18) THE CITY WILL NEVER BE INHABITED AGAIN "(51:26).

- THE UNGODLY NATIONS WOULD WEEP OVER THE DESTRUCTION OF BOTH BABYLONS (REV. 18; JER. 50:46).

- THE ISRAELITES WERE TO FLEE FROM BOTH BABYLONS (REV. 18:4; JER. 51:6).

- BOTH CITIES ARE DEPICTED AS GOLDEN CUPS FILLED WITH INIQUITIES FROM WHICH THE NATIONS HAVE DRUNK AND BECOME MAD (REV. 17:1-6; JER. 51:7)

- ALL HEAVEN REJOICES OVER THE DESTRUCTION OF BOTH (JER. 51:10,48; REV. 18:20).

- AFTER THE DESTRUCTION OF BOTH BABYLONS, ISRAEL WOULD SEEK THEIR GOD. THIS HAPPENED HISTORICALLY (EZRA I) AND IT WILL OCCUR IN THE FUTURE (ZECH. 13:9).

174

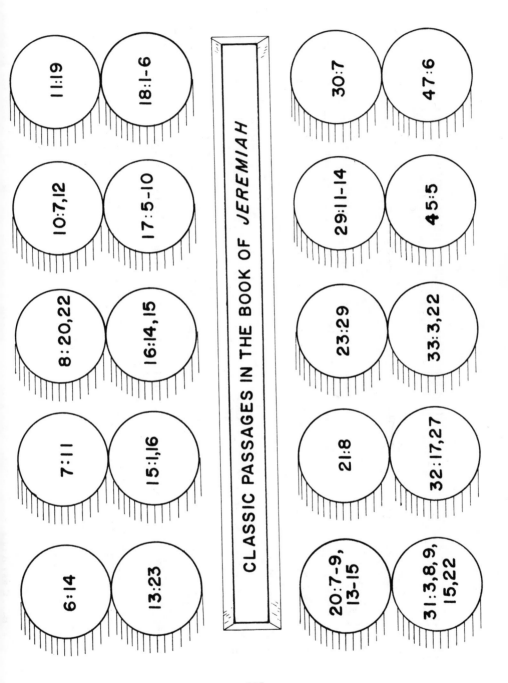

CLASSIC PASSAGES IN THE BOOK OF *JEREMIAH*

11:19

18:1-6

10:7,12

17:5-10

8:20,22

16:14,15

7:11

15:1,16

6:14

13:23

30:7

47:6

29:11-14

45:5

23:29

33:3,22

21:8

32:17,27

20:7-9, 13-15

31:3,8,9, 15,22

THE EIGHTEEN PROPHECIES

OF

JEREMIAH

- FALL OF JERUSALEM (1:14-16; 4:5-9; 5:15-17; 6:1-6; 32:2-3; 38:17-18)
- DESTRUCTION OF THE TEMPLE (7:11-15; 26:6-9)
- DEATH OF DEPOSED KING JEHOAHAZ IN EGYPT (22:10-12)
- UNLAMENTED DEATH OF KING JEHOIAKIM (36:27-30)
- CUTTING OFF OF THE ROYAL LINE OF KING JEHOIACHIN (22:24-30)
- DEATH OF TWO FALSE PROPHETS AND PUNISHMENT OF ANOTHER – ALL THREE LIVING IN BABYLON (29:20-32)
- DEATH OF A FALSE JERUSALEM PROPHET (28:13-17)
- CAPTURE AND EXILE OF A FRIEND NAMED SERAIAH (51:59)
- FAILURE OF THE EGYPTIAN-JUDEAN MILITARY ALLIANCE AGAINST BABYLON (37:5-10)
- DEFEAT OF EGYPT BY BABYLON AT CARCHEMISH (46:1-12)
- BABYLONIAN OCCUPATION OF EGYPT (43:9-13)
- SEVENTY YEAR CAPTIVITY OF JUDAH INTO BABYLON (25:11; 29:10)
- RESTORATION TO JERUSALEM AFTER THE 70 YEARS (27:19-22; 30:3, 10, 11, 18-21; 31:9, 12, 38, 39; 33:3-9)
- DEFEAT OF BABYLON AFTER THE 70 YEARS (25:12; 27:7)
- CAPTURE OF ZEDEKIAH (21:3-7; 34:1-5; 37:17)
- KINDLY TREATMENT OF THE GODLY EXILES IN BABYLON (24:1-7)
- FINAL REGATHERING OF PEOPLE OF ISRAEL (30:3, 10; 31:8-12)
- FINAL REBUILDING OF THE LAND OF ISRAEL (30:18-21; 31:38-39; 33:7-9)

176

# THE *NEW* COVENANT

- LOCATION: JEREMIAH 31:31-34

- RECIPIENTS: THE WHOLE HOUSE OF ISRAEL

- NATURE: ISRAEL TO RECEIVE NEW HEARTS FROM GOD·(24:7; 32:39)

- SUPERIORITY: IT WILL BE IMMUTABLE, UNCONDITIONAL, AND ETERNAL

- TIME PERIOD: AFTER THE TRIBULATION AND DURING THE MILLENNIUM

- BASIS: THE GRACE OF GOD AND THE DEATH OF CHRIST (HEB. 8:8-12)

- MEDIATOR: JESUS CHRIST! (30:9; 33:15-18)

BOOK OF

# LAMENTATIONS

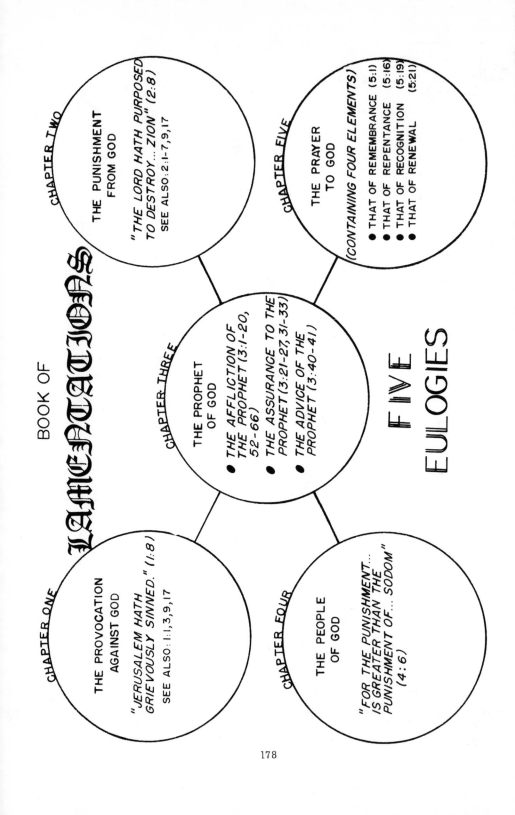

**CHAPTER ONE**

THE PROVOCATION
AGAINST GOD

"JERUSALEM HATH
GRIEVOUSLY SINNED." (1:8)

SEE ALSO: 1:1,3,9,17

**CHAPTER TWO**

THE PUNISHMENT
FROM GOD

"THE LORD HATH PURPOSED
TO DESTROY...ZION" (2:8)

SEE ALSO: 2:1-7,9,17

**CHAPTER THREE**

THE PROPHET
OF GOD

● THE AFFLICTION OF
THE PROPHET (3:1-20,
52-66)

● THE ASSURANCE TO THE
PROPHET (3:21-27, 31-33)

● THE ADVICE OF THE
PROPHET (3:40-41)

**CHAPTER FOUR**

THE PEOPLE
OF GOD

"FOR THE PUNISHMENT...
IS GREATER THAN THE
PUNISHMENT OF... SODOM"
(4:6)

**CHAPTER FIVE**

THE PRAYER
TO GOD

(CONTAINING FOUR ELEMENTS)

● THAT OF REMEMBRANCE (5:1)
● THAT OF REPENTANCE (5:16)
● THAT OF RECOGNITION (5:19)
● THAT OF RENEWAL (5:21)

FIVE
EULOGIES

# THE
# CAPTIVITY STAGE

## DANIEL         EZEKIEL

# THE BOOK OF **DANIEL**

# THE DIVINE DIET ①

**R**ESOLUTION: NOT TO EAT THE KING'S FOOD

**R**ECOMMENDATION: THAT A 10-DAY DIET BE CONDUCTED

**R**EWARD: DANIEL GRADUATES 10 TIMES SMARTER

# A STATUE AND A STONE ②

- THE FRUSTRATION OF THE BABYLONIANS: THE KING'S AIDES CANNOT INTERPRET HIS DREAM AND ARE SENTENCED TO DEATH.
- THE REVELATION OF THE LORD: GOD REVEALS THE DREAM TO DANIEL.
- THE INTERPRETATION OF THE PROPHET: DANIEL EXPLAINS THE DREAM.

| MATERIALS | BODY PARTS | WORLD POWER |
|---|---|---|
| GOLD | HEAD | BABYLON: 606-539 |
| SILVER | CHEST AND ARMS | PERSIA: 539-331 |
| BRASS | STOMACH AND THIGHS | GREECE: 331-323 |
| IRON AND CLAY | LEGS AND FEET | ROME: 322 B.C.-476 A.D. FUTURE |

NOTE: IN DAN. 7 THE SAME 4 NATIONS ARE DESCRIBED, BUT FROM A HEAVENLY VIEW, WHICH LOOKS UPON THEM AS 4 WILD ANIMALS.

| WORLD POWER | DESCRIPTION |
|---|---|
| BABYLON | LION |
| PERSIA | BEAR |
| GREECE | LEOPARD |
| ROME | MONSTER |

STATUE IS DESTROYED BY A GREAT STONE, WHICH REPRESENTS JESUS CHRIST!

- THE PROSTRATION OF THE KING: UPON HEARING THEIR INTERPRETATION NEBUCHADNEZZAR FALLS DOWN AND WORSHIPS DANIEL.

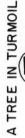

## A TREE IN TURMOIL Ⅳ

- THE TREE (NEBUCHADNEZZAR) CORRUPTED THROUGH VANITY

  1. NEBUCHADNEZZAR RELATES HIS DREAM TO DANIEL.
  2. DANIEL REVEALS THE DREAM TO NEBUCHADNEZZAR

- THE TREE (NEBUCHADNEZZAR) CORRECTED THROUGH INSANITY

  1. THE PRIDE OF NEBUCHADNEZZAR
  2. THE PUNISHMENT OF NEBUCHADNEZZAR
  3. THE PRAISE FROM NEBUCHADNEZZAR

## A FIERY FURNACE Ⅲ

- THE KING'S COMMAND: THAT ALL HIS LEADERS FALL DOWN AND WORSHIP A 90 FEET GOLDEN IMAGE. REASONS FOR THIS:
  1. TO ELEVATE HIS PERSON
  2. TO CONSOLIDATE HIS EMPIRE

- THE HEBREWS STAND: SHADRACH, MESHACH, AND ABEDNEGO REFUSE TO KNEEL AND ARE THROWN IN THE FIERY FURNACE

- THE LORD'S OWN MAN: CHRIST HIMSELF JOINS THE TRIO AND DELIVERS THEM OUT UNHURT.

*AND HE WALKS WITH ME, AND HE TALKS WITH ME...*

182

MENE MENE
TEKEL UPHARSIN

AN EVIL PLAN (6:1-9)
INSTIGATED BY SOME JEALOUS CHALDEANS TO TRAP DANIEL BY HIS DAILY PRAYER LIFE.

A KNEELING MAN (6:10-20)
DANIEL CONTINUES TO PRAY AND IS CAST INTO A DEN OF HUNGRY LIONS.

A HEAVENLY BAN (6:21-28)
DANIEL IS DELIVERED BY GOD'S ANGEL WHO SHUTS THE MOUTHS OF THE LIONS.

THE LIONS AND THE LION-HEARTED ⅥI

5:1
THE
BALL

5:5-6
THE
WALL

5:30-31
THE
FALL

5:2-4
THE
GALL

5:24-29
THE
SCRAWL
(WRITING)

5:7-23
THE
CALL

183

THE HEAVENLY HAND Ⅴ

*"AND FOUR GREAT BEASTS CAME UP FROM THE SEA..." (7:3)*
*"BEHOLD, ONE LIKE THE SON OF MAN CAME WITH THE CLOUDS... (7:13)*

| KINGDOM | SYMBOL | REPRESENTATIVE | |
|---|---|---|---|
| BABYLON 7:4 (2:37-38) | A LION | NEBUCHADNEZZAR | |
| PERSIA 7:5 (2:39) | A BEAR | CYRUS | |
| GREECE 7:6 (2:39) | A LEOPARD | ALEXANDER THE GREAT | |
| ROME 7:7-8 (2:40-43) | A ONE-HORNED MONSTER WITH TERRIBLE TEETH | HISTORICAL | ROMAN CAESARS |
| | | PROPHETICAL | ANTICHRIST |
| EVERLASTING KINGDOM 7:9-14 (2:44-45) | THE SON OF MAN | THE LORD JESUS CHRIST | |

*GODLESS KINGDOMS AND THE KINGDOM OF GOD*

(VII)

| SYMBOL | KINGDOM | REPRESENTATIVE | EVENT |
|---|---|---|---|
| A TWO-HORNED RAM 8:1-4,20 | MEDES AND PERSIANS | DARIUS III | • Some 250 Years in Advance Daniel Predicts the Resounding Defeat of DARIUS III at the Hands of ALEXANDER in 332 B.C. |
| A ONE-HORNED GOAT 8:5-8,21,22 | GREECE | ALEXANDER | • At ALEXANDER'S DEATH (Age 32) his Kingdom was Divided by his Four Generals.<br><br>LYSIMACHUS — ASIA MINOR<br>SELEUCUS — SYRIA<br>CASSANDER — GREECE<br>PTOLEMY — EGYPT |
| TWO LITTLE HORNED KINGS 8:9-20,23-27 | P A S T — SYRIA / F U T U R E — REVIVED ROMAN EMPIRE | ANTIOCHUS EPIPHANES / ANTICHRIST | Both to Conquer much (DAN. 8:9; REV. 13:4)<br>Both to Magnify Themselves (8:11; REV. 13:15)<br>Both Deceitful (8:25; 2 Thess. 2:10)<br>Both Offer a False Peace Program (8:25; I Thess. 5:2)<br>Both Hate and Persecute Israel (8:25; REV. 12:13)<br>Both Profane the Temple (8:11; MAT. 24:15)<br>Both Energized by Satan (8:24; REV. 13:2)<br>Both Active in Middle East for 7 Years (8:14; 9:27)<br>Both to Speak Against GOD (8:25; 2 Thess. 2:4)<br>Both to be Destroyed by GOD (8:25; REV. 19:19-20) |

THE HORNS OF THE HEATHEN (VIII)

## DANIEL: THE PRAYER OF A PROPHET

| | |
|---|---|
| TIME OF THE PRAYER | FIRST YR. OF PERSIAN RULE 538 B.C. (9:2) |
| OCCASION FOR THE PRAYER | DANIEL'S UNDERSTANDING OF JEREMIAH'S PROPHECY (9:2) |
| BASIS FOR THE PRAYER | THE PROMISE OF GOD (9:4) / THE MERCY OF GOD (9:9,18) |
| CONFESSION IN THE PRAYER | WE HAVE SINNED! (9:5,8,9,11,15,16) |
| REQUESTS IN THE PRAYER | THAT GOD WOULD BRING THEM OUT OF BABYLON AS HE ONCE DID OUT OF EGYPT (9:15) / THAT GOD WOULD FORGIVE (9:19) / THAT GOD WOULD ALLOW THE TEMPLE TO BE REBUILT IN JERUSALEM (9:16,17) |
| ANSWER TO PRAYER | "YEA, WHILE I WAS...IN PRAYER...GABRIEL...TOUCHED ME..."(9:21) |

## GABRIEL: THE PROPHECY OF AN ANGEL

| QUESTIONS | ANSWERS |
|---|---|
| • TO WHOM DOES THE PROPHECY REFER? | ISRAEL (9:24) |
| • WHAT ARE THE 70 WEEKS? | THEY REFER TO 7 SEVENS OF YEARS, OR, 490 YEARS. |
| • WHEN WOULD THIS PERIOD BEGIN? | AT THE REBUILDING OF JERUSALEM'S WALLS. MARCH 14, 445 B.C. |
| • WHAT ARE THE 3 TIME PERIODS WITHIN THE 70 WEEKS? WHAT HAPPENED DURING EACH PERIOD? | 7 "WEEKS" OR 49 YEARS — WALLS OF JERUSALEM TO BE REBUILT IN TROUBLOUS TIMES. FROM 445-396 B.C. |
| | 62 "WEEKS" OR 434 YEARS — MESSIAH TO BE CRUCIFIED. FROM 396 B.C. TO 32 A.D. |
| | **CHURCH AGE** |
| | 1 "WEEK" OR 7 YEARS — FROM RAPTURE – ARMAGEDDON. MINISTRY OF ANTICHRIST AND RETURN OF TRUE CHRIST. |

THE SECRET OF THE SEVENTY SEVENS

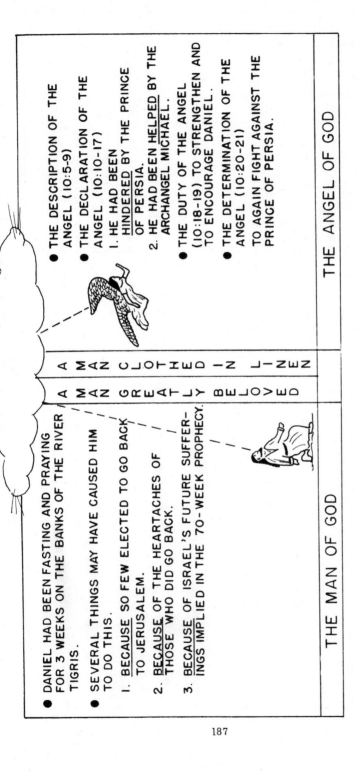

THE MAN OF GOD

- DANIEL HAD BEEN FASTING AND PRAYING FOR 3 WEEKS ON THE BANKS OF THE RIVER TIGRIS.
- SEVERAL THINGS MAY HAVE CAUSED HIM TO DO THIS.
  1. BECAUSE SO FEW ELECTED TO GO BACK TO JERUSALEM.
  2. BECAUSE OF THE HEARTACHES OF THOSE WHO DID GO BACK.
  3. BECAUSE OF ISRAEL'S FUTURE SUFFERINGS IMPLIED IN THE 70-WEEK PROPHECY.

A MAN CLOTHED IN LINEN
A MAN GREATLY BELOVED

THE ANGEL OF GOD

- THE DESCRIPTION OF THE ANGEL (10:5-9)
- THE DECLARATION OF THE ANGEL (10:10-17)
  1. HE HAD BEEN HINDERED BY THE PRINCE OF PERSIA.
  2. HE HAD BEEN HELPED BY THE ARCHANGEL MICHAEL.
- THE DUTY OF THE ANGEL (10:18-19) TO STRENGTHEN AND TO ENCOURAGE DANIEL.
- THE DETERMINATION OF THE ANGEL (10:20-21) TO AGAIN FIGHT AGAINST THE PRINCE OF PERSIA.

THE CONFLICT ABOVE THE CLOUDS (X)

11:1-20     11:21-35     11:36-45

| ALEXANDER AND PREDECESSORS | ANTIOCHUS EPIPHANES | ANTICHRIST |
|---|---|---|
| THIS AMAZING CHAPTER CONTAINS NO LESS THAN 38 FULFILLED PROPHECIES. SOME ARE AS FOLLOWS: | ● HE WAS A CRUEL, JEW-HATING SYRIAN KING WHO OCCUPIED JERUSALEM FOR AWHILE, RULING FROM 175-164 B.C. | ● WILL BE TOTALLY SELF-WILLED |
| ▲ THE RULE OF 4 PERSIAN KINGS (V.2) | ● ON SEPT. 6, 171 B.C. HE BEGAN HIS BLASPHEMOUS ACTIONS AGAINST THE TEMPLE. | ● WILL MAGNIFY HIMSELF AND MALIGN GOD. |
| ▲ THE WAR OF THE 4th WITH GREECE | | ● WILL PROSPER FOR AWHILE |
| ▲ THE RISE AND FALL OF ALEXANDER (V.3-4) | ● THE SUPREME INSULT TOOK PLACE ON DEC 15, 168 WHEN HE SACRIFICED A HUGE SOW ON THE JEWISH TEMPLE ALTAR. | ● WILL NOT REGARD THE GODS OF HIS FATHERS |
| ▲ THE 4-FOLD DIVISION OF HIS EMPIRE (V.4) | | ● WILL HAVE NO DESIRE FOR WOMEN |
| ▲ THE EVENTUAL ALLIANCE OF TWO OF THESE TWO KINGDOMS (V.6) | ● IN THREE DAYS HE MURDERED OVER 40,000 JEWS. | ● WILL HONOR THE GOD OF FORTRESS |
| ▲ THE EGYPTIAN PLUNDER OF SYRIA (V.8) | | ● WILL BE ATTACKED BY TWO SOUTH-ERN AND NORTHERN KINGS |
| ▲ THE UNSUCCESSFUL RETALIATION OF SYRIA (V.9) | ● ON DEC. 25, 165 (2300 DAYS AFTER THE SEPT. 6, 171 DATE, SEE DAN. 8:9-14) SOME JEWISH HEROES CALL-ED THE MACCABEES RECAPTURED JERUSALEM AND THE SYRIAN OCCUPATION ENDED. | ● WILL OCCUPY THE HOLY LAND |
| ▲ THE CIVIL WAR IN EGYPT (V.14) | | ● WILL OCCUPY EGYPT |
| ▲ THE SYRIAN OCCUPATION OF PALESTINE (V.16) | | ● WILL HEAR FRIGHTFUL NEWS WHILE IN EGYPT |
| ▲ THE TEMPLE DESECRATION BY A SYRIAN KING (V.31-32) | | ● WILL RETURN TO THE HOLY LAND AND WAGE WAR |
| ▲ THE MACCABEAN REVOLT (V.32) | | ● WILL BE DESTROYED BY CHRIST ON MT. ZION |
| ▲ THE EVENTUAL DEFEAT OF THE MACCABEANS (V.33) | | |

A CHRONOLOGY OF CHRISTLESS KINGS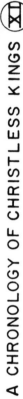

**"....A TIME OF TROUBLE, SUCH AS NEVER WAS..." (12:1)**

| | |
|---|---|
| ● THE HELPER IN THE TRIBULATION | MICHAEL THE ARCHANGEL (12:1) |
| ● THE LENGTH OF THE TRIBULATION | THERE ARE THREE SPECIFIC TIME PERIODS LISTED HERE CONCERNING THE TRIBULATION AND FOLLOWING EVENTS. |

| 1260 DAYS (12:7) | 1290 DAYS (12:11) | 1335 DAYS (12:12) |
|---|---|---|
| – A REFERENCE TO THE FINAL AND WORST PART OF THE TRIBULATION, SOME 3 1/2 YEARS. | – A REFERENCE TO THE FIRST TIME PERIOD PLUS 30 DAYS. THIS TIME MAY BE NEEDED TO CONDUCT THE VARIOUS JEWISH, GENTILE AND ANGELIC JUDGMENTS. | – A REFERENCE TO THE SECOND TIME PERIOD PLUS 45 DAYS. THIS MAY BE SPENT IN PREPARING FOR THE MILLENIAL GOVERNMENT. |

| | |
|---|---|
| ● THE INTEREST CONCERNING THE TRIBULATION | BOTH ANGELS AND O.T. PROPHETS (12:5-8) |
| ● THE SALVATION DURING THE TRIBULATION | ".... EVERY ONE ...WRITTEN IN THE BOOK." (12:1) "MANY SHALL BE PURIFIED, AND MADE WHITE...." (12:10) |
| ● THE SIGNS PRECEEDING THE TRIBULATION | AN INCREASE IN SPEED (12:4) |
| | AN INCREASE IN KNOWLEDGE (12:4) |
| ● THE RESURRECTIONS FOLLOWING THE TRIBULATION (12:2-3) | AT BEGINNING OF MILLENNIUM — RESURRECTION OF O.T. AND TRIBULATION SAINTS |
| | AT END OF MILLENIUM — RESURRECTION OF ALL UNSAVED DEAD |

THE COMING CALAMITY

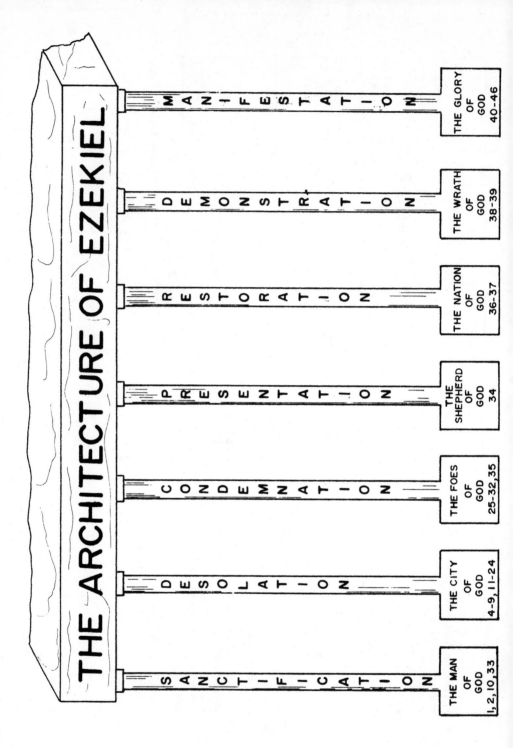

THE ARCHITECTURE OF EZEKIEL

SANCTIFICATION — THE MAN OF GOD — 1, 2, 10, 33

DESOLATION — THE CITY OF GOD — 4-9, 11-24

CONDEMNATION — THE FOES OF GOD — 25-32, 35

PRESENTATION — THE SHEPHERD OF GOD — 34

RESTORATION — THE NATION OF GOD — 36-37

DEMONSTRATION — THE WRATH OF GOD — 38-39

MANIFESTATION — THE GLORY OF GOD — 40-46

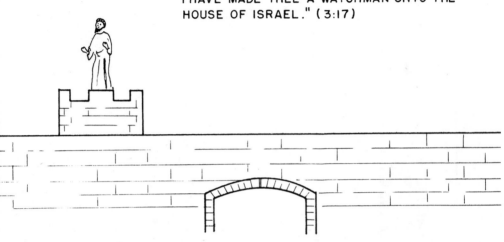

" I HAVE MADE THEE A WATCHMAN UNTO THE HOUSE OF ISRAEL." ( 3:17 )

WHAT HE SEES

| THE VISION OF THE LIVING CREATURES |
| --- |
| • THEIR IDENTITY: THEY ARE ANGELIC CHERUBIMS (10:20)<br>• THEIR DESCRIPTION: THEY HAD THE FACE LIKENESS OF A <u>LION</u>, AN <u>OX</u>, A <u>MAN</u> AND AN <u>EAGLE</u> (1:10) |

WHAT HE HEARS

| THE VOICE OF THE LIVING GOD |
| --- |
| • TELLING HIM TO WARN THE WICKED TO CEASE THEIR EVIL WORKS (3:18-19)<br>• TELLING HIM TO WARN THE RIGHTEOUS TO CONTINUE THEIR GOOD WORKS (3:20-21) |
| HE WAS TO TOTALLY ABSORB THE MESSAGE OF GOD ( 3:1-2 ) |

# THE SANCTIFICATION OF THE MAN OF GOD
## —EZEKIEL—
(1,2.10,33 )

| 12 SYMBOLIC ACTS | 6 PARABLES | 12 MESSAGES |
|---|---|---|
| • DRAWING A MAP OF JERUSALEM (4:1-3) | • A FRUITLESS VINE TREE (15:1-8) | • 6:1-14 |
| • LAYING ON HIS LEFT SIDE FOR A PORTION OF 390 DAYS (4:4-5) | • THE ADOPTED GIRL WHO BECAME A HARLOT (16:1-63) | • 7:1-27 |
| • LAYING ON HIS RIGHT SIDE FOR A PORTION OF OF 40 DAYS (4:6) | • THE TWO EAGLES (17:1-21) | • 13:1-23 |
| • PREPARING A SCANT MEAL (4:9-17) | • THE TENDER TWIG (17:22-24) | • 14:1-12 |
| • SHAVING HIS HEAD AND BEARD (5:1-4) | • THE MOTHER LIONESS AND HER CUBS (19:1-9) | • 14:13-23 |
| • STAMPING HIS FEET AND CLAPPING HIS HANDS (6:11) | • THE TWO HARLOT SISTERS (23:1-49) | • 18:1-32 |
| • DIGGING THROUGH A WALL (12:1-16) | | • 20:1-44 |
| • TREMBLING AS HE ATE HIS FOOD (12:17-20) | | • 20:45-49 |
| • SLASHING ABOUT WITH A SWORD (21:9-17) | | • 21:1-7 |
| • DRAWING A MAP OF THE MIDDLE EAST (21:18) | | • 22:1-16 |
| • BOILING A POT OF WATER DRY (24:1-24) | | • 22:17-22 |
| • REMAINING TEARLESS AT HIS WIFE'S FUNERAL (24:15-18) | | • 22:23-31 |

*HIS EXTENDED TEMPLE VISIT 8-11*

• HE SEES THE DEPARTURE OF JUDAH FROM THE GLORY OF GOD.

• HE SEES THE DEPARTURE OF THE GLORY OF GOD FROM JUDAH.

NOTE: WHILE IN EXILE EZEKIEL WARNS HIS FELLOW CAPTIVES THAT JERUSALEM, ALREADY OCCUPIED BY THE BABYLONIANS, WOULD LATER BE TOTALLY DESTROYED. HE USES DRAMA, PARABLES, AND SERMONS TO EMPHASIZE THIS WARNING.

# THE DESOLATION OF THE CITY OF GOD
# —JERUSALEM—
(4-9,11-24)

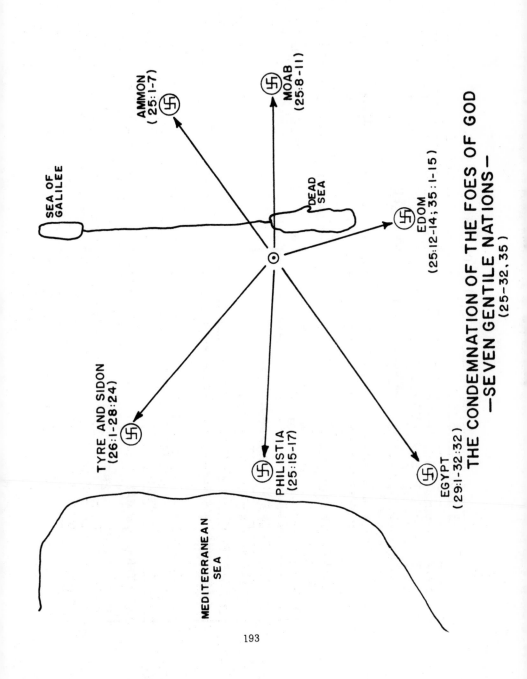

SEA OF GALILEE

AMMON
(25:1-7)

MOAB
(25:8-11)

DEAD SEA

EDOM
(25:12-14; 35:1-15)

TYRE AND SIDON
(26:1-28:24)

PHILISTIA
(25:15-17)

EGYPT
(29:1-32:32)

MEDITERRANEAN SEA

THE CONDEMNATION OF THE FOES OF GOD
—SEVEN GENTILE NATIONS—
(25-32, 35)

(ADDITIONAL INFORMATION ON TYRE AND EGYPT)

| | TYRE (26-28) | EGYPT (29-32) |
|---|---|---|
| **HISTORY** | • WAS GREATEST COMMERCIAL CITY IN O.T. TIMES<br><br>• KING OF TYRE HELPED BOTH DAVID AND SOLOMON DURING THEIR REIGNS. | • TO BE DESOLATE FOR 40 YEARS.<br><br>• TO REMAIN AS A MINOR KINGDOM.<br><br>• TO BE NEVER SOUGHT OUT BY ISRAEL FOR HELP AGAIN.<br><br>• TO BE PUNISHED DURING THE TRIBULATION. |
| **LOCATION** | • TYRE WAS ACTUALLY TWO CITIES, ONE ON THE MEDITERRANEAN, AND THE OTHER NEARLY A MILE ON AN ISLAND IN THE SEA ITSELF. | |
| **SIN** | • PRIDE AND GROSS MATERIALISM | |
| **RULER** | • ETHBAAL II (DURING EZEKIEL'S TIME) | |
| **PUNISHMENT** | • BOTH CITIES TO BE DESTROYED, NEVER TO BE REBUILT.<br><br>• AREAS THEN TO BECOME BARE, A PLACE FOR THE SPREADING OF FISHING NETS. | |
| **SINISTER FORCE BEHIND TYRE** | • MANY BELIEVE GOD IS ACTUALLY CONDEMNING AND DESCRIBING SATAN IN 28:11-19.<br><br>• HE WAS THE REAL POWER BEHIND ITS SIN. | |

| THE MANY FALSE SHEPHERDS | | THE ONLY TRUE SHEPHERD |
|---|---|---|
| • THEY FED THEMSELVES INSTEAD OF THE FLOCK (34:2-3) | I | • HE WOULD SEARCH OUT THE LOST SHEEP (34:11) |
| • THEY HAD NOT TAKEN CARE OF THE WEAK, NOR TENDED THE SICK, NOR BOUND UP THE BROKEN BONES, NOR SOUGHT THE LOST.(34:4) | AM | • HE WOULD DELIVER THEM FROM THEIR ENEMIES (34:12) |
| • THE SHEEP WERE THEN SCATTERED HAVING NO SHEPHERD. (34:5) | THE | • HE WOULD GATHER THEM FROM ALL NATIONS (34:13) |
| • THEY HAD BECOME PREY TO THE WILD ANIMALS (34:5) | GOOD | • HE WOULD FEED THEM UPON THE MOUNTAINS OF ISRAEL (34:14) |
| • THEREFORE, THE SHEHERDS WOULD BE PUNISHED (34:9) | SHEPHERD | • HE WOULD GIVE THEM REST IN GREEN PASTURES (34:15) |
| • THEIR POSITIONS AS SHEPHERDS WOULD BE REMOVED (34:9) | | • HE WOULD PUT SPLINTS AND BANDAGES UPON THEIR BROKEN LIMBS. (34:16) |
| • THEY WOULD NOT BE THEMSELVES FED BY THE GREAT SHEPHERD. (34:9-10) | | • HE WOULD HEAL THE SICK (34:16) |
| • THEY WOULD BE JUDGED AND DESTROYED (34:16) | | • HE WOULD ESTABLISH DAVID AS HIS TRUSTED UNDERSHEPHERD (34:23)(SEE ALSO EZEK. 37:24; JER. 30:9; HOS. 3:5) |
| | JN. 10:11 | • HE WOULD MAKE AN ETERNAL PACT WITH THEM (34:25) |
| | | • HE WOULD GUARANTEE THEIR SAFETY AND PLACE THEM IN A PERFECT PARADISE (34:25-28) |

# THE PRESENTATION OF THE SHEPHERD OF GOD
## —JESUS CHRIST—

34

## REASONS FOR

- TO PUNISH THE FOES OF ISRAEL (36:1-7)
- TO EXONERATE THE NAME OF GOD (36:20-23)

## SYMBOL OF

- EZEKIEL CARVES THE NAME JUDAH ON ONE STICK AND EPHRAIM ON ANOTHER (37:15-16)
- HE THEN HOLDS BOTH STICKS IN ONE HAND, INDICATING GOD WOULD SOMEDAY RE-UNITE ALL 12 TRIBES (37:17-20)

## NECESSITY OF

- ISRAEL WAS OUT OF THE PROMISED LAND BECAUSE OF SIN (36:17-19)

## VISION EXPLAINING

- EZEKIEL SPEAKS TO A VALLEY FILLED WITH DRIED ISRAELI BONES (37:1-6)
- THE BONES JOIN TOGETHER AND ARE COVERED WITH FLESH (37:7-8)
- HE SPEAKS AGAIN AND THE BREATH OF LIFE ENTERS THEIR BODIES (37:9-14)

## RESULTS OF

- ISRAEL TO ONCE AGAIN BECOME GOD'S PEOPLE (36:28;37:27)
- TO BE SPRINKLED WITH CLEAR WATER (36:25)
- TO POSSES THE INDWELLING HOLY SPIRIT (36:27)
- TO BE GIVEN NEW HEARTS (36:26)
- TO HAVE A NEW TEMPLE (37:26,28)
- TO BE RULED OVER BY DAVID (37:24)
- TO BE JUSTIFIED AMONG THE NATIONS (36:30)
- TO HAVE ABUNDANT CROPS (36:29,30,34,35)
- TO REPOPULATE JERUSALEM AND OTHER WASTE CITIES (36:38)
- TO OCCUPY THE HOLY LAND FOREVER (37:25)

# THE RESTORATION OF THE NATION OF GOD
## -ISRAEL-
36,37

## I — IDENTITY OF THE INVADERS

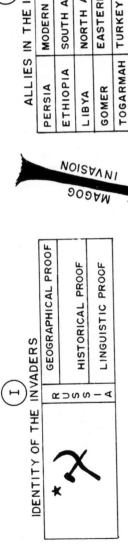

| R U S S I A | GEOGRAPHICAL PROOF |
| | HISTORICAL PROOF |
| | LINGUISTIC PROOF |

## II — ALLIES IN THE INVASION

| PERSIA | MODERN IRAN |
| ETHIOPIA | SOUTH AFRICAN NATIONS |
| LIBYA | NORTH AFRICAN NATIONS |
| GOMER | EASTERN EUROPE |
| TOGARMAH | TURKEY |

MAGOG INVASION

## III — REASONS FOR THE INVASION

- TO CASH IN ON THE RICHES OF ISRAEL (38:11,12)
- TO CHALLENGE THE AUTHORITY OF THE ANTICHRIST (DAN. 11:40-44)

## IV — RESULTS OF THE INVASION

- RUSSIA TOTALLY DEFEATED BY GOD (38:21-23)
- FIVE-SIXTHS OF THE RUSSIAN TROOPS DESTROYED ON THE MOUNTAINS OF ISRAEL (39:2)
- SEVEN YEARS TO BE SPENT IN BURNING THE WAR WEAPONS (38:9)
- SEVEN MONTHS IN BURYING THE DEAD (38:12)

# THE DEMONSTRATION OF THE WRATH OF GOD
## —RUSSIA—
### 38,39

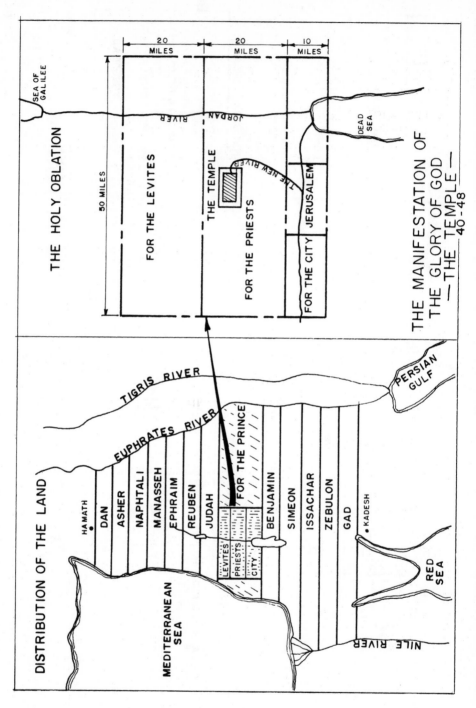

THE HOLY OBLATION

20 MILES | 20 MILES | 10 MILES

SEA OF GALILEE

JORDAN RIVER

50 MILES

FOR THE LEVITES

THE TEMPLE

THE NEW RIVER

FOR THE PRIESTS

DEAD SEA

JERUSALEM

FOR THE CITY

THE MANIFESTATION OF
THE GLORY OF GOD
— THE TEMPLE —
40 - 48

DISTRIBUTION OF THE LAND

TIGRIS RIVER

EUPHRATES RIVER

PERSIAN GULF

HAMATH

DAN
ASHER
NAPHTALI
MANASSEH
EPHRAIM
REUBEN
JUDAH

FOR THE PRINCE

LEVITES
PRIESTS
CITY

BENJAMIN
SIMEON
ISSACHAR
ZEBULON
GAD

KADESH

MEDITERRANEAN SEA

RED SEA

NILE RIVER

# FACTS ON THE MILLENNIAL TEMPLE ─

| | |
|---|---|
| • ITS BIBLICAL ORDER | (1) THE TABERNACLE OF MOSES (EXOD. 40) <u>DATES</u>: 1444-1100 B.C. |
| | (2) THE TEMPLE OF SOLOMON (I KINGS 6) <u>DATES</u>: 959-586 B.C. |
| | (3) THE TEMPLE OF ZERUBBABEL (EZRA 6) NOTE: THIS WAS LATER GREATLY ENLARGED BY HEROD. SEE JN. 2 <br><br> <u>DATES</u>: 516 B.C. TO 70 A.D. |
| | (4) THE TEMPLE OF CHRIST'S BODY (JN. 2) <u>DATES</u>: 4 B.C. TO 30 A.D. |
| | (5) THE SPIRITUAL TEMPLE, THE CHURCH (ACTS 2) <u>DATES</u>: PENTECOST - RAPTURE <br> • THE WHOLE CHURCH (EPH. 2:21) <br> • THE LOCAL CHURCH (I COR. 3:16,17) <br> • THE INDIVIDUAL BELIEVER (I COR. 6:19) |
| | (6) THE TRIBULATIONAL TEMPLE (REV. 11) <u>DATES</u>: RAPTURE - ARMAGEDDON |
| | (7) THE MILLENNIAL TEMPLE (EZEK. 40-48) <u>DATES</u>: THROUGH THE MILLENNIUM |
| • ITS PURPOSE | (1) TO PROVIDE A PLACE FOR THE GLORY CLOUD OF GOD (EZEK. 43) |
| | (2) TO PROVIDE A CENTER FOR THE KING OF GLORY (43:7) |
| • ITS PRIESTHOOD | THOSE PRIESTS FROM THE LINE OF ZADOK (40:46) |

- **ITS PRINCE**
  1. DEFINITELY NOT CHRIST. SEE 45:22; 46:16
  2. PERHAPS SOMEONE FROM THE LINE OF DAVID.

- **ITS UNIQUE FEATURES**
  1. NO VEIL
  2. NO TABLE OF SHEWBREAD
  3. NO LAMPSTANDS
  4. NO ARK OF THE COVENANT
  5. EAST GATE TO BE CLOSED (44:2)

- **ITS SACRIFICES**
  ( ISA. 56:7; 60:7; JER. 33:18; ZECH. 14:16-20)
  1. AS A <u>REMINDER</u> TO ALL OF THE NECESSITY OF THE NEW BIRTH.
  2. AS AN <u>OBJECT LESSON</u> OF THE COSTLINESS OF SALVATION.
  3. AS AN <u>EXAMPLE</u> OF THE AWFULNESS OF SIN.
  4. AS AN <u>ILLUSTRATION</u> OF THE HOLINESS OF GOD.

- **ITS RIVER**
  (47:1-12)
  1. THE <u>SOURCE</u>: PROCEEDING FROM BENEATH THE TEMPLE.
  2. THE <u>COURSE</u>: FLOWS TO DEAD SEA AND MEDITERRANEAN SEA.
  3. THE <u>FORCE</u>: WATERS TO SWIM IN!

- **ITS CITY**
  1. CIRCUMFERENCE: SIX MILES (48:35)
  2. NAME: THE MILLENNIAL JERUSALEM WILL BE NAMED, JEHOVAH-SHAMMAH, MEANING, "THE LORD IS THERE" (48:35)

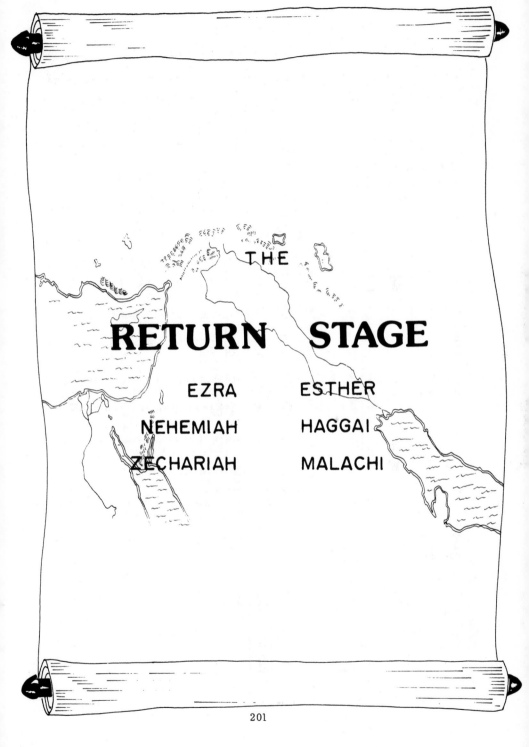

THE

RETURN STAGE

EZRA ESTHER

NEHEMIAH HAGGAI

ZECHARIAH MALACHI

*"For thus saith the LORD, After seventy years are accomplished at Babylon, I will visit you, and perform my good word toward you, in causing you to return even unto this place." (JER. 29:10)*

| FOREIGN KING | DATE | EVENT | SCRIPTURE | O.T. BOOK | LOCATION |
|---|---|---|---|---|---|
| CYRUS THE GREAT | 539-530 | CONQUERS BABYLON | DAN. 5 | • EZRA 1-6 | |
| | | ISSUES RETURN DECREE | EZRA 1-3 | | JERUSALEM |
| CAMBYSES | 530-522 | NOT REFERRED TO IN O.T. | — | • HAGGAI | |
| SMERDIS | 522-520 | STOPS WORK ON THE TEMPLE | EZRA 4:1-23 | • ZECHARIAH | |
| DARIUS THE GREAT | 520-486 | ORDERS WORK TO CONTINUE | EZRA 4:24; 6:1-22 | (See Ezra 5:1; 6:14) | |
| AHASUERUS | 486-465 | MAKES ESTHER HIS QUEEN | ESTHER 1-10 | • ESTHER | PERSIA |
| ARTAXERXES | 465-424 | ALLOWS EZRA TO RETURN | EZRA 7-12 | • EZRA 7-12 | JERUSALEM |
| | | ALLOWS NEHEMIAH TO RETURN | NEHEMIAH 1-13 | • NEHEMIAH | |

# A CHRONOLOGY OF THE RETURN STAGE

# SIX SOVEREIGN TRIPS

"By the rivers of Babylon, there we sat down, yea, we wept, when we remembered Zion." (Psa. 137:1)

| THREE TRIPS FROM JERUSALEM TO BABYLON | | | | |
|---|---|---|---|---|
| DATE | CAPTIVES | O.T. PROPHETS | | FOREIGN KINGS |
| 606 | DANIEL | IN BABYLON | DANIEL | BEFORE 539 | NEBUCHADNEZZAR BELSHAZZAR |
| 597 | EZEKIEL | | EZEKIEL | | |
| 586 | ZEDEKIAH | IN JERUSA-LEM | JEREMIAH | AFTER 539 | KING CYRUS AND HIS GENERAL DARIUS |

JORDAN

EUPHRATES

"When the LORD turned again the captivity of Zion, we were like them that dream." (Psa. 126:1)

| THREE TRIPS FROM BABYLON TO JERUSALEM | | | |
|---|---|---|---|
| DATE | LEADER | FOREIGN KING | O.T. PROPHET |
| 536 | ZERUBBABEL AND JOSHUA | • CYRUS THE GREAT | HAGGAI |
| | | • CAMBYSES | |
| | | • SMERDIS | ZECHARIAH |
| | | • DARIUS THE GREAT | |
| 455 | EZRA | ARTAXERXES | EZRA |
| 445 | NEHEMIAH | ARTAXERXES | NEHEMIAH |

# THE BOOK OF EZRA

## PERIOD UNDER ZERUBBABEL (1-6)

### PROCLAIMING — THE KING

- CYRUS SIGNS THE RETURN DECREE (1:1-4)
- A SPIRITUAL JEWISH MINORITY RESPOND TO THIS (1:5-11). SOME 40,000 NOW LEAVE FOR JERUSALEM

### RECLAIMING — THE PEOPLE

- THEY RECLAIM THEIR GENEAOLOGY (2)
- THEY RECLAIM THEIR THEOLOGY (3) UPON REACHING JERUSALEM THE ALTAR IS BUILT AND THE FEASTS ARE KEPT.

### DEFAMING — THE DEVIL

- HE ATTEMPTED COMPROMISE (4:1-3)
- HE ATTEMPTED SLANDER (4:4-24)

### SUSTAINING — THE LORD

- THROUGH THE MINISTRY OF HAGGAI AND ZECHARIAH (5:1; 6:14)
- THROUGH THE TITLE DEED SEARCH BY KING DARIUS (6)

---

50 YEAR GAP

EVENTS IN BOOK OF ESTHER TAKE PLACE

---

## PERIOD UNDER EZRA (7-10)

### FROM THE KING (7) — COOPERATION

- EZRA IS HELPED BY KING ARTAXERXES WHO ENCOURAGES THE JEWS TO GO AND WRITES LETTERS IN THEIR BEHALF.

### FOR THE TRIP (8) — PREPARATION

- EZRA GATHERS 1500 FAMILIES PLUS 300 LEVITICAL PRIESTS.
- HE COLLECTS FIVE MILLION DOLLARS.
- HE OBSERVES A TIME OF PRAYER AND FASTING.

### BY THE SCRIBE (9) — SUPPLICATION

- HE LEARNS THE PEOPLE HAD ALREADY COMPROMISED THEIR TESTIMONY.
- HE POURS OUT HIS SOUL IN PRAYER TO GOD OVER THEIR SIN.

### OF THE PEOPLE (10) — PURIFICATION

- THEY ARE CONVICTED OF THEIR SINS.
- THE PEOPLE PUT AWAY THEIR SINS.

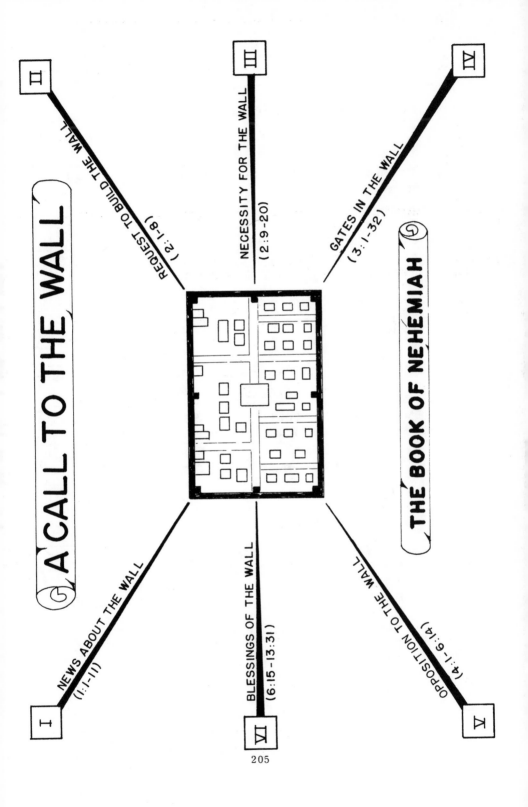

A CALL TO THE WALL

THE BOOK OF NEHEMIAH

I  NEWS ABOUT THE WALL
(1:1-11)

II  REQUEST TO BUILD THE WALL
(2:1-8)

III  NECESSITY FOR THE WALL
(2:9-20)

IV  GATES IN THE WALL
(3:1-32)

V  OPPOSITION TO THE WALL
(4:1-6:14)

VI  BLESSINGS OF THE WALL
(6:15-13:31)

205

## THE NEWS CONCERNING THE WALL (1:1-11)

- THE PROBLEM: THE JEWS IN JERUSALEM COULD NOT GET THE WALL UP.

- THE PRAYER:
  1. NEHEMIAH OFFERS UP A CONFESSION TO GOD OVER THE EVIL DEEDS OF THE JEWS.
  2. NEHEMIAH OFFERS UP INTERCESSION TO GOD OVER THE EARNEST NEEDS OF THE JEWS.

## THE REQUEST TO BUILD THE WALL (2:1-8)

- NEHEMIAH ASKS AND RECEIVES PERMISSION TO RETURN AND BUILD UP THE WALLS OF JERUSALEM.

## THE NEED FOR AND THE TRIP AROUND THE WALL (2:9-20)

- FOR PROTECTION: TO KEEP THE OUTSIDERS OUT.

- FOR SEPARATION: TO KEEP THE INSIDERS IN.

- HIS MIDNIGHT RIDE: "AND I WENT OUT BY NIGHT" (2:13)

- HIS MID-MORNING RALLY: "LET US BUILD UP THE WALL" (2:17)

THE TEN GATES IN THE WALL

SHEEP GATE 3:1 — A TYPE OF THE CROSS
FISH GATE 3:2 — A TYPE OF SOULWINNING
OLD GATE 3:6 — A TYPE OF THE OLD NATURE
VALLEY GATE 3:13 — A TYPE OF SUFFERING
DUNG GATE 3:14 — A TYPE OF THE FLESH

FOUNTAIN GATE 3:15 — A TYPE OF HOLY SPIRIT
WATER GATE 3:26 — A TYPE OF WORD OF GOD
HORSE GATE 3:28 — A TYPE OF WARFARE
EAST GATE 3:29 — A TYPE OF RAPTURE
MIPHKAD GATE 3:31 — A TYPE OF BEMA JUDGMENT

THE OPPOSITION TO THE WALL

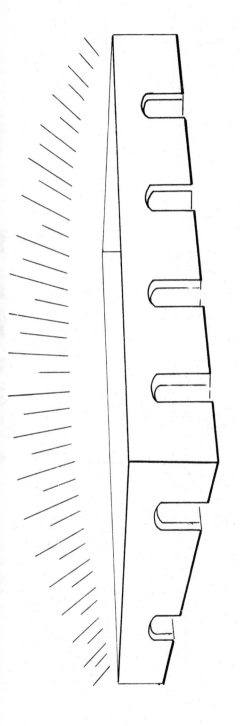

THE *READING* OF THE WORD OF GOD (8:1-8;9:3)

THE *RESTORATION* OF THE FEAST OF TABERNACLES (8:13-18)

THE *PRAYER RECITATION* OF ISRAEL'S HISTORY (9:6-38)

THE *RATIFICATION* OF A SPECIAL COVENANT (9:38,10:1-39)

THE *REPOPULATING* OF THE CITY OF DAVID (11:1,2)

THE *RENOUNCING* OF SINS (9:1-2)

THE *REJOICING* OF ALL THE REMNANT (8:12)

THE BLESSINGS OF THE COMPLETED WALL

## THE RISE OF ESTHER

**CHAPTERS 1-2**

THE REJECTION OF VASHTI: KING AHASUERUS DIVORCES HIS WIFE VASHTI WHILE DRUNK.

THE SELECTION OF ESTHER: ESTHER IS THE WINNER OF A BEAUTY CONTEST AND BECOMES HIS NEW QUEEN.

THE DETECTION OF MORDECAI: HE OVERHEARS AND REPORTS A PLOT TO ASSASSINATE THE KING.

## THE LIES OF HAMAN

**CHAPTERS 3-5**

INFERNAL SERVITUDE: HAMAN IS APPOINTED PRIME MINISTER AND INSTIGATES A PLOT TO KILL ALL THE JEWS. HE THUS BECAME ONE OF SATAN'S MOST LOYAL O.T. SLAVE.

INTESTINAL FORTITUDE: UPON HEARING OF THIS WICKED PLOT, BOTH MORDECAI AND ESTHER DISPLAY GREAT COURAGE AND WISDOM.

- AS SEEN BY MORDECAI'S ADVICE TO ESTHER
- AS SEEN BY ESTHER'S APPEARANCE BEFORE THE KING.

## THE PRIZE OF FAITH

**CHAPTERS 6-10**

THE EXECUTION OF A BEAST—HAMAN!
- SCENE ONE: THE KING'S BEDROOM. HE LEARNS OF MORDECAI'S LOYALTY.
- SCENE TWO: THE KING'S BANQUET HALL. HE LEARNS OF HAMAN'S TREACHERY.

THE INSTITUTION OF A FEAST—PURIM!

## THE BOOK OF ESTHER

| DATE AND CONTENT OF MESSAGE | DIRECTION OF MESSAGE |
|---|---|

## FIRST MESSAGE

| S | M | T | W | T | F | S |
|---|---|---|---|---|---|---|
| (1) | 2 | 3 | 4 | 5 | 6 | 7 |
| 8 | 9 | 10 | 11 | 12 | 13 | 14 |
| 15 | 16 | 17 | 18 | 19 | 20 | 21 |
| 22 | 23 | 24 | 25 | 26 | 27 | 28 |
| 29 | 30 | | | | | |

**AUGUST – 520 B.C.    1:1-15**

### PERFORM:
- DON'T GIVE UP!
  - ON THE TEMPLE.
- DO GO UP!
  - ON THE MOUNTAIN.
- GET ALL STIRRED UP!
  - ABOUT THE LORD.

TO THE HAND!

## SECOND MESSAGE

| S | M | T | W | T | F | S |
|---|---|---|---|---|---|---|
| | | 1 | 2 | 3 | 4 | 5 |
| 6 | 7 | 8 | 9 | 10 | 11 | 12 |
| 13 | 14 | 15 | 16 | 17 | 18 | 19 |
| 20 | (21) | 22 | 23 | 24 | 25 | 26 |
| 27 | 28 | 29 | 30 | | | |

**SEPTEMBER – 520 B.C.    2:1-9**

### PATIENCE:
- IN SPITE OF THE INSIGNIFICANT TEMPLE THEY HAD JUST BUILT.
- BECAUSE OF THE MAGNIFICANT TEMPLE THEY SOMEDAY WOULD BUILD.

TO THE HEART!

## THIRD MESSAGE

| S | M | T | W | T | F | S |
|---|---|---|---|---|---|---|
| | | 1 | 2 | 3 | 4 | |
| 5 | 6 | 7 | 8 | 9 | 10 | 11 |
| 12 | 13 | 14 | 15 | 16 | 17 | 18 |
| 19 | 20 | 21 | 22 | 23 | (24) | 25 |
| 26 | 27 | 28 | 29 | 30 | | |

**NOVEMBER 520 B.C.    2:10-23**

### PONDER:
- THE FACT OF JUDAH'S CONTAMINATION (2:10-17)
- THE FACT OF GOD'S DETERMINATION (2:18-19)
- THE FACT OF THE COMING TRIBULATION (2:20-22)
- THE FACT OF ZERUBBABEL'S ELEVATION (2:23)

TO THE HEAD!

BOOK OF HAGGAI

211

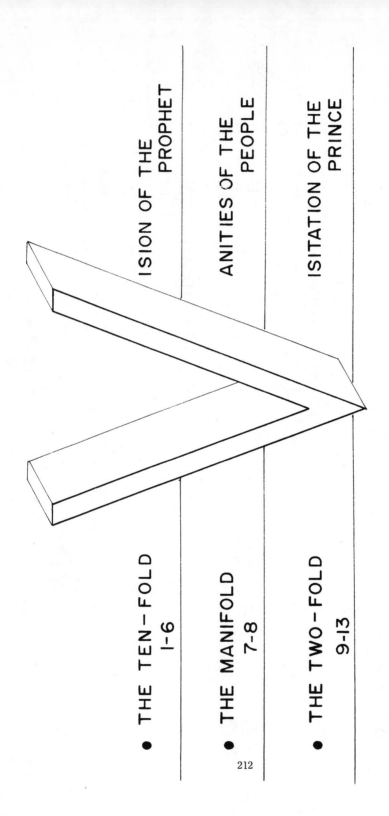

THE BOOK OF ZECHARIAH

● THE TEN-FOLD
ISION OF THE
PROPHET
1-6

● THE MANIFOLD
ANITIES OF THE
PEOPLE
7-8

● THE TWO-FOLD
ISITATION OF THE
PRINCE
9-13

# THE TEN VISIONS

| | DESCRIPTION | EXPLANATION | | |
|---|---|---|---|---|
| ONE | *RIDER ON A RED HORSE (1:7-17)* | • AN APPEARANCE OF CHRIST HIMSELF, ALONG WITH SOME ANGELS, KEEPING WATCH OVER JERUSALEM. | | |
| TWO | *THE FOUR HORNS (1:18-19)* | • MAY REPRESENT THE FOUR GENTILE WORLD POWERS WHICH SCATTERED (OR WOULD SCATTER) ISRAEL<br><br>1. ASSYRIA (Captured Northern kingdom)<br>2. BABYLON (Captured Southern Kingdom)<br>3. PERSIA (Plot Against ALL Jews. See Esther)<br>4. ROME (Has and will Scatter Israel) | | |
| THREE | *THE FOUR ARTISIANS (1:20-21)* | • A PROBABLE REFERENCE TO THE FIRST FOUR SEALED JUDGMENTS IN REV. 6:1-8 | | |
| FOUR | *MAN WITH A MEAS- URING LINE (2:1-13)* | • REFERENCE TO THE MEASURING OF JERUSALEM DURING THE MILLENNIUM (EZEK. 40:1-5; 48:30-35) | | |
| FIVE | *THE CONFRONTATION IN HEAVEN (3:1-10)* | THE CHARGE | The wearing of filthy garments | |
| | | THE CHARGED | Joshua and the people of Jerusalem | |
| | | THE PROSECUTOR | SATAN | |
| | | THE DEFENDER<br><br>↓<br><br>JOSHUA<br><br>CLEANSED<br>AND<br>REASSURED | THE BRANCH! called this 4 times in O.T. | |
| | | | The Branch of David (ISA.11:1; JER.23:5; 33:15) | Gospel Fulfill- ment Matthew! |
| | | | My Servant, The Branch (Zech.3:8) | Gospel Fulfill- ment Mark! |
| | | | The Man Branch (Zech. 6:12) | Gospel Fulfill- ment Luke! |
| | | | The Branch of Jehovah (Isa. 4:2) | Gospel Fulfill- ment John! |

| | DESCRIPTION | EXPLANATION | | |
|---|---|---|---|---|
| **SIX** | THE GOLDEN LAMPSTAND AND THE TWO OLIVE TREES (4:1-14) | ● HISTORICAL MEANING | May Refer to the Anointed Team of Zerubbabel and Joshua | |
| | | ● PROPHETICAL MEANING | May Refer to the Anointed Team of Elijah and Moses. See Rev. 11:3-12 | |
| **SEVEN** | THE FLYING SCROLL (5:1-4) | ● MEANING | GOD'S JUDGMENT Upon the Land. Man had Broken HIS Entire Moral Law. | |
| | | ● REASON | SIN of Swearing | AGAINST GOD | VERTICAL |
| | | | SIN of Stealing | AGAINST MAN | HORIZONTAL |
| **EIGHT** | THE WOMAN IN THE EPHAH (5:5-11) | ● THE WOMAN | A Type of Sin and Rebellion | |
| | | ● THE COVER | A Type of GOD'S Restraining Power | |
| | | ● THE DESTINATION | To Establish itself in Babylon | |
| | | | Organized Rebellion | Had begun here (Gen. 11) |
| | | | Organized Rebellion | May end here (Rev. 18) |
| **NINE** | THE FOUR CHARIOTS (6:1-8) | ● FOUR HEAVENLY SPIRITS (ANGELS) ARE DRIVING THESE CHARIOTS, PROCEEDING FROM TWO BRASS MOUNTAINS | | |
| | | ● THE CHARIOTS MAY REPRESENT THE FIRST 4 PLAGUES OF REV. 6 AND THE MOUNTAINS THE JUDGMENT OF GOD | | |
| **TEN** | THE CROWNING OF JOSHUA (6:9-15) | ● ZERUBBABEL DOES THIS TO ILLUSTRATE THE 3-FOLD MINISTRY OF THE COMING MESSIAH  1. He would build the Temple  2. He would minister as a Priest  3. He would rule as a King | | |

214

## QUESTION

WOULD IT BE POSSIBLE TO SET ASIDE ONE OF ISRAEL'S APPOINTED DAYS OF FASTING ?

## ANSWER

IT WAS ISRAEL'S CARELESSNESS CONCERNING THIS VERY THING THAT CAUSED THE BABYLONIAN CAPTIVITY.

## CONCLUSION

THEY WERE TO OBSERVE THE FAST DAYS WITH HEART-FELT DEVOTION.

# ZECHARIAH
# AND THE
# PEOPLE

| HIS FIRST | COMING |
|---|---|

- HE COMES TO FEED THE FLOCK OF GOD (11:7)

- HE IS REJECTED BY ISRAEL'S LEADERS (11:8)

- HE THUS SET ASIDE ISRAEL (11:10)
  - POSSIBLE MEANING OF HIS BREAKING THE STAFF CALLED BEAUTY.

- HE MAKES HIS TRIUMPHAL ENTRY INTO JERUSALEM (9:9)

- HE IS SOLD FOR 30 PIECES OF SILVER (11:12)

- HE PREDICTS THE DESTRUCTION OF JERUSALEM (11:14)
  - POSSIBLE MEANING OF HIS BREAKING THE STAFF CALLED BAND.

- HE IS CRUCIFIED (12:10)

**THE TWO VISITATIONS OF THE PRINCE**

| HIS SECOND | COMING |
|---|---|

- THE CRUEL REIGN OF THE ANTICHRIST (11:16)

- JERUSALEM TO BE SURROUNDED AND TAKEN (14:2)

- TWO THIRDS OF THE JEWS TO PERISH (13:8)

- ONE THIRD OF THE JEWS TO BE SAVED (13:9)

- CHRIST TO APPEAR UPON THE MOUNT OF OLIVES (14:4,8)

- ARMAGEDDON TO BE FOUGHT (12:3; 14:2,3)

- GOD'S ENEMIES TO BE DESTROYED (12:4,9; 14:12-15)

- ISRAEL TO RECOGNIZE CHRIST (12:10-14)

- ISRAEL TO BE CLEANSED (13:1)

- ISRAEL TO BE SETTLED IN THE LAND (10:6-12; 8:8)

- GENTILES TO WORSHIP THE LORD (14:16-19)

- JERUSALEM TO BE FILLED WITH HAPPY BOYS AND GIRLS (8:5)

- CHRIST TO BUILD THE TEMPLE (6:13)

- CHRIST TO RULE AS THE PRIEST - KING OVER ALL THE WORLD (6:13; 9:10)

# ZECHARIAH AND THE PRINCE

# THE LOVE OF GOD

| HIS LOVE STATED | HIS LOVE SCORNED | HIS LOVE SHOWN |
|---|---|---|
| "I HAVE LOVED YOU, SAITH THE LORD... I LOVED JACOB, AND I HATED ESAU" (1:2-3)<br><br>A TWO-FOLD PROBLEM IS SEEN IN THESE VERSES<br>●WHY GOD "HATED" ESAU! NOTE:<br>  I. THE GENESIS ACCOUNT (25,27) NEVER RECORDS GOD HATING ESAU.<br>  2. THE HEBREW WORD HERE TRANSLATED HATE CAN ALSO MEAN PREFERENCE SEE GEN. 29:31; PROV. 14: 20; LK. 14:26.<br>  3. THE NAME ESAU ALSO DOUBTLESS STOOD FOR THE ENTIRE WICKED NATION OF EDOM, WHOSE WAYS GOD DID INDEED HATE!<br><br>●WHY GOD LOVED JACOB! THIS IS THE <u>REAL</u> PROBLEM IN THE PASSAGE! | ●BY THE PROPHETS<br>  I. WHO CHEATED <u>THE LORD</u> THROUGH THEIR SHABBY OFFERINGS (1:7-8)<br>  2. WHO CHEATED <u>THE PEOPLE</u> THROUGH THEIR SORRY EXAMPLE. (2:7-9)<br><br>●BY THE PEOPLE:<br>  I. THROUGH THEIR INEQUALITIES (2:10)<br>  2. THROUGH THEIR INTERMARRIAGES (2:11)<br>  3. THROUGH THEIR IMMORALITY (2:14)<br>  4. THROUGH THEIR INSINCERITY (2:17)<br>  5. THROUGH THEIR INDEBTEDNESS (3:8-10)<br>  6. THROUGH THEIR INCRIMINATIONS (3:13-15) | ●BY REMEMBERING HIS SAINTS (3:16)<br>●BY SENDING HIS OWN SON.<br>  I. HIS <u>FIRST COMING</u> WAS INTRODUCED BY JOHN THE BAPTIST (3:1a)<br>  2. HIS <u>SECOND COMING</u> WILL BE INTRODUCED BY ELIJAH THE PROPHET (4:5)<br><br>THE PURPOSE OF HIS SECOND COMING<br><br>● REGARDING THE GENTILES:<br>TO CONSUME THEM AS CHAFF IN HIS OVEN (4:1,3)<br>● REGARDING THE JEWS:<br>→ THEY WILL ACCEPT CHRIST! (3:1b)<br>→ THEY WILL BE GATHERED BY CHRIST! (3:17)<br>→ THEY WILL BE PURIFIED BY CHRIST! (3:2-3)<br>→ THEY WILL BE HEALED BY CHRIST! (4:2) |

## THE BOOK
### OF
# Malachi